The Midlife Crisis Survival Kit

Everything you need to know to successfully
negotiate this life challenge

Russell Wickens

For Janie, Tilly and Bella

Acknowledgements

For someone who thinks he lives a life of solitude and works alone most of the time,
I seem to have come into contact with a great many wonderful people who were
prepared to give me their help, guidance, support and general encouragement
along the way. This undertaking was made a lot easier through working
with you all - thank you.

For Carole Gaskell who was my first real coach and mentor, for Dr. Michael Anthony
in the US and Chris Barrow here in the UK, many grateful thanks.

Also, for Michelle at Ashridge for your patient listening and then prompt delivery of great
illustrations, for Amy Yap Day who never once questioned why I could not
complete the most simple of computer literate tasks by myself and Choppa for the
final formatting and cover design.

And to Janie – an inspirational example of authenticity, creative energy
and unwavering support.

Chinese Ideogram for "Crisis"

Danger

Opportunity

INTRODUCTION

Change   (v) To make or become different; (of the Moon) to arrive at a fresh phase; become new; (n) the action of changing; an instance of becoming different.

Crisis   (n) A time of intense difficulty and danger; the turning point of a disease when an important change takes place, indicating either recovery or death.

Chaos   (n) Complete disorder and confusion (origin C15 denoting a gaping void).

****

Answer these questions:

Are you aged between 35 and 50?	Y/N
Has your life turned out the way you expected it to?	Y/N
Are you generally unhappy?	Y/N
Do you experience prolonged periods of hopelessness?	Y/N
Are you having the life you want?	Y/N
Have the reference points for your life achievements changed?	Y/N
Do you question your values?	Y/N
Do you ever feel like your life is falling apart?	Y/N
Are you unsure that this is the "right" life for you?	Y/N
Do you get feelings that Life is pointless?	Y/N
Do you seek gratification or happiness in transient things?	Y/N
Do old roles no longer fit so well?	Y/N
Do people tell you that you seem different?	Y/N
Do you have a general sense of uneasiness?	Y/N
Is there an urgency about life that wasn't there before?	Y/N
Do the bigger questions of life trouble you? (Why am I here? etc.)	Y/N
Has Time become more precious?	Y/N
Do you ever ask yourself "Is this it...?"	Y/N

If you have answered "Yes" to the first question and to more than half of the following questions, there is a strong likelihood that you are experiencing symptoms of a mid-life transition or what has become very commonly known as the "mid life crisis". This period when intense introspection accompanied by some collision of circumstance causes us to re-examine our lives, at its very centre begins to question the validity and sustainability of our existence. As we subject all areas of our lives to close scrutiny in a search for more meaning, around us the whole structure is usually either threatening to collapse, or already has. This book, while providing some context for the phenomenon of Mid Life Crisis, has a very specific practical application and purpose: to engage the reader in the process of mid life transition, helping them to understand the rigours of its tests and then to accelerate them towards the holy grail of its benefits - learning, wisdom, growth and most important.....happiness.

If you want to use this experience as a positive for your life, find meaning in the process of transition and to more quickly re-orient yourself afterwards to take full advantage of this testing period in your life, read on. This book is for you.

ROAD MAP AND HOW TO USE THIS BOOK

To give you a clear idea of the shape of your journey, I have based the structure of this book on an existing three-stage transition model. This is to help you at least give form to something that in many other ways may defy this kind of formalised description. However, this does not mean that we have slavishly tried to force a new understanding into an old mould. Many different models have been created before and since by psychologists to give form to a picture that identifies the true nature of transition at mid life. However, few others allow the same latitude for an individual's journey as this will. As interpreted here, its prescriptive nature fades away and leaves us with a template that can be applied to any of you willing to both commit fully to your journey and undergo the analytical scrutiny that this implies. I hope that person is You.

Here is the route that we take.

PART 1 – THE END/BEGINNING

A look at the map of mid life transition and the route you are taking

Understanding of the concept of mid life change - Who, What, When and Why

– The context of Mid Life Crisis

Underpinning the philosophy for going forward - Re-frame of Being, Doing and Having

The nature of "Crisis" -   Is this it?!

– Questioning the fulfilment and sustainability of our existence

– Identify where YOU are on the map

The nature of Surrender

The pursuit of Authenticity – What does it really mean?

- Do you know what you want to express about yourself?

- The notion of individuation

Pursuit of self actualisation -   Establishing a hierarchy of needs

- Your personal Needs, identifying them, getting them met

- Boundaries and Standards, protecting yourself

- The difference between Needs and Musts

Expressing Authenticity - The roles you play – do you still want to?

- So WHAT do you really want for your life....?

Fear and Acceptance – what lies on the other side of fear?

- Making yourself vulnerable to the World

Recognition and Dismantling to achieve renewal – growth through change

- embracing the concept of the cycle

Seeking meaning

PART 2 – THE NEUTRAL ZONE

Moving away from "magical thinking"

Exploring and being in the Neutral Zone - engagement – your active participation

– discovering mastery - the myth of Beowulf

Expressing your personal Values and leading an authentic life

The difference between Needs and Values – expressing them

The nature of Purpose   –   aligning with purpose

-    defining your life Purpose

-    establishing Hierarchies of Purpose to support you

-    draw your own Pyramid of Purpose

Additional tools to reinforce the context of your progress

Standing on the threshold - The nature of responsibility and forgiveness

- Dismantlement – time to re-build the edifice of your life

PART 3 – THE NEW BEGINNING

The journey towards renewal

Discovering and exploring your creativity

Who are you now?

Exercises to establish your self-awareness

-    write your own obituary

-    3RD person assessment

Moving through - Create your own rite of passage

- What do you REALLY want?

Clarify the details - Mind mapping

               - Summarise your satisfactions and dissatisfactions

Establishing the bigger picture - Idealising your future and projecting into it

               - Goal setting

               – Vision > Mission > Goal

               - Future timeline

Foundation Tools   –   Dust Bust your Life

               -    Tolerations

               -    Wheel of Life

               -    Self care

               -    Flow activities

Your own erupting volcano – time to make the earth shake

This book is designed to be a workbook with practical tools for you to use. The aim is to assist you in painting a new picture of you and your life. As you navigate your way through these testing waters, you will increase your self-understanding and awareness. This book will help you to decide what the future YOU can look like. Complete the assessments and make notes as you go along. Do not be afraid to journal experiences or jot down private thoughts as you go through. Once you have finished reading this you will have an emerging picture of yourself. Continue to refer back and add to this. See it almost like a photographic montage of your journey. It will prove to be one of the most valuable and insightful periods of your life.

PART 1

The End and the Beginning

"Man does not form a part of his environment; on the contrary, he always finds himself in an attitude of facing up to it. The act of living is the having to do something so that our surroundings shall not annihilate us. This living then constitutes a problem, a question, a difficulty to be resolved."
- Jose Ortega y Gasset:

"When you get to the end of all the light you know it's time to step into the darkness of the unknown. Faith is knowing that one of two things shall happen: either you will be given something solid to stand on, or you will be taught how to fly."
- Edward Teller

"The best way out is through"
- Ralph Waldo Emerson

****

Here is a dream:

'It was night in some unknown place, and I was making slow and painful headway against a mighty wind. Dense fog was flying along everywhere. I had my hands cupped around a tiny light, which threatened to go out at any moment. Everything depended on my keeping the little light alive. Suddenly I had the feeling that something was coming up behind me. I looked back and saw a gigantic black figure following me. But at the same moment I was conscious in spite of my terror that I must keep my little light going through night and wind, regardless of all dangers. When I awoke I realised at once that the figure was my own shadow on the swirling mists, brought into being by the little light I was carrying. I knew too that this little light was my consciousness, the only light I have. Though indefinitely small and fragile in comparison with the powers of darkness, it is still a light, my only light.[4]

How do you feel reading that.....?

The popular label of crisis is one that sticks, very simply because despite any rational explanation, to all of us as individuals when it happens, it is usually just that – a crisis. We find ourselves in intensely painful life circumstances that lack an obvious solution. The same usually financial or social parameters need to be maintained, our entire status quo is under threat, the values that have supported us thus far now look decidedly flimsy and no one is supplying any answers.

There have been some very creditable efforts over the decades to help us understand the concept of mid life change. In fact, mid life transition has been the subject of close psychological scrutiny for a long time. Psychologists like Jung, (whose dream is described above), philosophers, authors and researchers have dissected their own and other people's bewildering life journeys. Many have made detailed attempts at understanding the crisis that many find themselves in when they reach the stage of life that the Spanish philosopher Ortega y Gasset calls "Initiation". At just the point when we could all be sitting back and making a satisfied assessment of our progress so far, we

---

often find ourselves instead lamenting the emptiness and lack of fulfillment in our lives. Frequently, we feel caught in a growing maelstrom of uncertainty, or worse still witnesses to the wreckage of what was once our lives, now inexplicably lying in ruins around us.

Crisis can only be handled when it is perceived as essential to growth rather than a complication to be avoided. This as both an understanding and applied practice is key to recovery and true transcendence, as we shall see later. Of course the concept of "enjoying the journey not the destination" comes as slim comfort to those that having arrived at this point see themselves involved in nothing short of survival. As the tide begins to cover the island where they once lived, they look around the shrinking surface area in vain for something that will keep them afloat. The decision they face of course, is not where to stay, but how to leave – and when/if they do, where are they headed for...?

Those attempts to help us understand the phenomenon of transition at mid life, usually offer us psychological rationale illustrated by real life examples, without the comfort of exactly what to do. Everyone's experience is intensely different and although comparison helps, it does not beat understanding support. Without exception, any client who ever came to me with transition issues, has had a highly developed desire to both understand what they are experiencing as well as declaring the will to go through it. However, while both of these components are essential, the way ahead is never clear. The third necessary component is the unwavering support that they receive from a coach in both re-designing the way the life they want to lead and then taking the action steps to achieve it. The tools provided here can provide the same sound basis for you to do just that. This and the knowledge that if you don't quit you **will** win and that by surrendering to the flow of this raging current, you will be cast into calm water on the other side a great deal sooner if you have the tools and self awareness to help you. You may feel alone, but you are not on your own. While everyone's journey is as unique as the individual gifts they have to offer, do take comfort from the fact that you are neither the first nor the last person to feel this way. Those that have preceded you moved on as a result of what they learned about themselves. You will do the same if you can accept where you are and see this as a process for good.

WHO, WHAT, WHEN AND WHY...?

Essentially what this book is setting out to do for you is to describe and deal with a handful of very simple things: What, Who, When and Why. Or...what is Mid Life Crisis? Who does it affect? When does it happen? And Why not only does it happen, but Why also is it something that we find ourselves almost completely unprepared for? The obvious sequential addition to the series is "How" – how do we deal with and transcend the most challenging era of our lives. The tools for this and how to apply them are available to you throughout the book.

Those same books that attempt to bring reason and form to the nature of transition, also comprehensively attempt to define the kind of people it affects. Looked at objectively, our lives are unquestionably a *series* of transitions and within those parameters we can be further sub-categorised into different types of people that experience and go through them. The main thrust of this book is not to venture too deeply into this need for categorisation, but rather to acknowledge its validity as one of many tools that can help our understanding. If we accept that our lives <u>are</u> a series of transitions, there will always be a valid process of refinement that attempts to sort those transitioning individuals into groups of age, culture, class, education and conditioning of one kind or another. For our purposes here, we will not make any in depth analysis of this, but rather concentrate on the common factors that emerge. To do this implies rigorous objectivity, so let us apply that. My purpose here is to help you help yourself in the most effective way possible. Use the descriptions, diagrams and tools to identify and plot your own position. Awareness of where you are and how you are will be key to your progress later.

BE DO HAVE – A RE-FRAME

What often shows up behaviourally in people engaged in the early stages of transition, is a progressive focus on "Doing" in order to disguise or distract from an unravelling that is too frightening to contemplate. Career paths are pursued more vigorously in pursuit of the same things that so far have failed to deliver the anticipated satisfaction. Houses, partners, spouses and lovers may all be changed in an effort to re-instil joy. The successful career woman having given it all up to raise her children now stands on a new threshold. Does she re-enter the fray, joining a world where once she was comfortable, but where new technology and procedures may invalidate her experience? Or does she go to the gym and shut out her fear on the exercise bicycle, focus dotingly on the achievements of her children to the exclusion of her own, or go shopping in search of retail therapy...? Does her husband who is exactly where he wanted to be 15 years ago in terms of his career and his material achievements, admit to despising his job and his boss, thereby negating not only the last 15 years of work, but also his choices and desires? Or is that more painful than having an affair with his secretary?

The above are cliched and over simplistic generalisations and certainly do no justice to the paralysing fears and tumultuous emotional state of people who arrive at this point. However, they serve as a good example of the avoidance that is so easy to engage in to postpone the inevitable acknowledgement:

"I am not happy...."

So while the majority of those people experiencing dissatisfaction on such a grand scale engage in a state of increased activity to shut out the noise in their heads, what emerges? Well, as their paralysing fear around changing the status quo prevents a detached evaluation, they simply DO more, in ignorance of the fact that BEING in its purest sense is what they crave. We live in a hectic world, lived at a furious pace with a focus that is very much on "Doing" certain things in order to "Have" the things that we want in order that we will then "Be" happy. This model does two things that do not serve us. It puts our happiness at a place in the future, based entirely on the deferred gratification that we expect to receive when certain criteria have been met – the car, the house, the promotion, the salary increase, the holiday etc. So our happiness is never in the present moment and never will be for as long as we keep it at arm's length. The second thing it does is to de-prioritise our essential selves and our values. What we are saying is: If I DO these things, then I'll HAVE these things, then I'll BE happy. Consider this radical re-frame instead:

- If I am able to BE the person that I want to be, which requires me to be completely authentic and express the values that are important to me.
- Then that will require that I DO whatever is necessary to achieve and sustain that state.
- Which will mean that I will HAVE the things that I want.

I understand just how challenging that thought might be to some of you. Those of you with established career structures, domestic commitments, relationships to consider and myriad other concerns that now appear inextricably interwoven into the fabric of your lives, may well throw up your arms and say it can not be done. For now, just hold the thought that it might. We will return to this theme throughout the book and I hope that by the end you may have revised this early response. For those of you to whom this sounds like oxygen to a drowning man, you will need no convincing.

CRISIS

According to the philosopher Jose Ortega y Gasset, crisis occurs when we find that the convictions which previously supported our world view are no longer admissible and so we no longer know what to think. In the absence of new beliefs to replace the old ones, we are left without either compass or map. Disdain for the now outmoded old values, does nothing to help the establishing of new ones. Through our socialised natures and the need to understand our world by preconceived criteria, we lose sight of what we truly think or believe. Crisis occurs when the need to shake this off and express ourselves individually becomes overwhelming.

Ortega y Gasset's natural conclusion in his assessment of crisis is that Man reaches a state that can only be described as desperation:
"...although he (Man) must do something in order to live – we know that living is the condition of having to do something – he finds no occupation that satisfies him; nor do the matters on his material and social horizon or the ideas on his intellectual horizon

20

move him to anything which seems satisfactory. He will go on doing this or that; but he will do it like an automaton, without achieving any sense of solidarity between himself and his acts; these acts he considers valueless, of no account, without meaning. When this happens there surges up in him an unconquerable loathing of the world and of living, both of which seem to him to have a character which is purely negative."

Does any of that resonate with you? Ortega y Gasset's seminal work was written nearly fifty years ago. Yet the essence of what he describes has not changed at all given my own experience as a Coach with clients. He goes on to describe how when Man feels the valueless and negative character of his existence, his first reaction is to resolve it by making one part of it secure. This is a very familiar scenario. I would state categorically that great success was never achieved by insuring against failure. Yet there are a staggering number of people who see essential change and going forward as being possible only when they have qualified for their pension! The inner call to some greater and more fulfilling purpose put on hold while securing it to some financial anchor. How many men have denied themselves a path of more authentic expression while they wait for a pension, bonus, the children's school fees to be paid or the mortgage redeemed? The need for security though, understandable as it is, can delay or even prevent the exploration of a life of substance. It is one of many tests that I am sure you recognise.

Ortega y Gasset goes on to describe Man's yearning for simplicity, or a return to the primitive past and a turning away from complicated culture. In its most extreme form this is what he calls "returning to oneself", a re-encounter with one's real truth and an abandonment of those positions or stimuli that mask it. Have you ever found yourself yearning for a simpler existence? Are there friends or acquaintances who may even have taken the momentous step of downsizing their lives in pursuit of a life closer to Nature. There are stock brokers and traders that I have encountered as clients, who have been more than content to leave behind the fat bonuses and adrenalised greed culture of their working lives and seek to find a more earthed existence at mid life. Tending the orchard or vineyard they have planted, learning carpentry, raising livestock or any one of so many occupations, this is really a pursuit of re-connection. It embodies an application to something more fulfilling that comes at mid life to those who feel this disconnection at a visceral level. They may not be able to articulate it, but they do feel it.

For most of us the turbulence and drama of a mid life crisis take place over a number of years, hallmarked by those nagging questions of "Is this it? Is this all there is to look forward to?" To others, our friends and family, the external signs are all too obvious: relationships breaking down, drama-fuelled affairs, workplace-related dissatisfactions and their own concomitant frictions. Internally though, the restive anger and confusion are symptoms of a deeper, more profound anxiety. We may be reaching a watershed that marks the end of growing up and the start of growing old, but do we understand it? We often sense intuitively the momentousness of the change we are caught up in. However, the sheer size and weight of its implications usually engender a fear that is paralysing. All the security that accompanies our life plans is gone because there is no longer a life plan. The comforting linear progression of life, job, family, career has been erased like a chalk mark from a blackboard, leaving in its place an ill-defined smudge. Where the assumption of our lives between early thirties and late forties showed the interest on our previous investment of time and energy being cheerfully banked, now instead we deal with a crash with all stock value wiped out. The crisis of the mid life transition blows apart the cherished fantasy that adulthood would be an orderly, linear, competent progression between the half-forgotten dramas of adolescence and an as yet only dimly conceived senility.

We cannot afford to ignore the primacy of our inner world, nor its need for unique and authentic self-expression. To do so is to invite a shrinking of our essential selves, a contraction of our nature – premature decay. The psychologist Jung himself describes his own mid life transition as a crisis that tested him severely. Yet it was only through fully engaging with his own fear of the unknown and the pain that accompanied his process that he finally unearthed the rich seam of creativity that characterised his later working life. His own summation mirrors my own: that to deny or avoid the growth of this essential process through fear of the pain, will entail the missed opportunity of real growth and creativity and the chance to find out just how uniquely powerful we are. We will follow the same circular path, passing the same familiar landmarks of crumbling life structure, feeling the same overwhelming anger, alienation and stunted expression. The choice is very simple but stark: break out of the current or be sucked into the vortex.

WHERE ARE YOU ON THE MAP?

Take a look at the diagram on the next page. It is a Mid Life Transition Model that charts the common course of Transition at mid life and allows you to make an assessment of your own position. What the model demonstrates clearly is that progression through all three zones of End/Beginning, Neutral Zone and New Beginning requires a transition from passivity to active involvement which will of its own volition become self-perpetuating as momentum is gained. Once you have moved beyond this stage, personal performance levels improve as well. As you can see, through active engagement in the process and seeking to move forward, you break free from the potential cycle of denial and alienation that keeps you stuck in the pit of chaos. This active engagement will be supported by the tools that are available for your use along the way. They provide both a focus and a support structure to keep your motivation high.

By modelling the course that research shows to be the norm however, we run the risk of reducing the experience of Mid Life Transition to a lowest common denominator diagram that endeavours to shoe-horn all participants into a convenient pattern. This is profoundly not the intention. The aim here is to demonstrate simply that there are elements of predictability that will correlate with your own experience, however intensely personal and painful that might be. The nature of the circumstances that brought you here or that you are now enduring are impossible to generalise beyond the critical components of self-abandonment and loss of "creative" involvement in your life in a generic sense. Nurse these thoughts as you plot your position on the model. Your progress through these turbulent waters requires that you engage actively in your journey, while at the same time trying to find out who you are now and to re-define yourself accordingly.

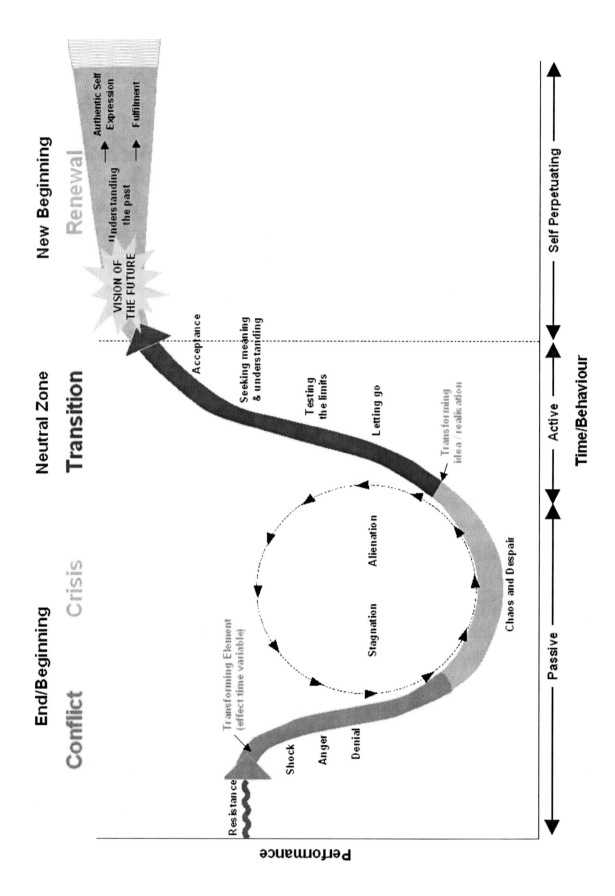

End/Beginning

Conflict

Crisis

Neutral Zone

Transition

New Beginning

Renewal

Performance

Resistance

Transforming Element (effect time variable)

Shock

Anger

Denial

Chaos and Despair

Stagnation

Alienation

Transforming idea / realisation

Letting go

Testing the limits

Seeking meaning & understanding

Acceptance

VISION OF THE FUTURE

Understanding the past

Authentic Self Expression

Fulfilment

Passive

Active

Self Perpetuating

Time/Behaviour

If you examine the diagram closely, you will see that immediately prior to the first Transforming Element, life will have been uncomfortable. The resistance that precedes it may have been going on for months or even years before the dam breaks. It is just as likely that the affected individual will have been in deep denial about their satisfaction and happiness levels as it is that they will have been fully cognisant and complaining. Everyone's unique experience will be just that. But if you scratch the surface you will find evidence of rumbling discontent deep in the Earth that has been presaging the inevitable disaster for a long time. Whatever form the crisis takes, this is the inevitable and unavoidable point that insists on change. Re-alignment to your true self and how you express that to the outside world is key to your being able to negotiate this territory effectively.

This is not to say that there is a quick fix. Our evolution and the lesson that we learn (and have to learn) along the way, requires that at a cellular level we absorb the experience fully. Somehow our journey requires that we do not miss out a stage. What we can do though is to avoid repeatedly sliding back into the vortex of stagnation and despair that typifies deep crisis. Fundamental changes are made by transcending the unwillingness or inability to make them. Everything that you want lies just outside your comfort zone. The "engagement" that I refer to is the decision to change – and to take the first step towards the fulfilment of authenticity.

The biggest challenge for the moment though is not even engagement in the pursuit of an authentic future. It is acceptance and surrender.

SURRENDER

Surrender does not imply passivity. Far from it. Acceptance of your profound needs now is only a surrender to the primacy of your soul's journey. Such acceptance requires a very active participation in order to achieve its fullest expression. You are in full pursuit of absolute authenticity and as such this will require a measure of action. Such a journey can come at very high cost. Not to engage with this now will simply see you back on the wheel of crisis. Understand the notion of "surrender" better as a giving in to and acceptance of the process. Paradoxical as this might sound, if you were swimming and letting the current take you, this would not imply a willingness to drown! On the contrary, you would continue swimming, aided by the impetus that the force of the current gave you. In the same way, you are simply investing the journey with a measure of trust that allows you to relinquish control. In pursuit of your authenticity you need not restrict the outcome of your future to what is known. Rather you can trust in the greater potential of the unknown. Possibility becomes infinite through not being foreshortened by logic; great success was never achieved through reason alone. It requires faith and trust. And for your eyes to be open.

The alchemists maintained that we could only create in our own image, that the form of new creation was reliant on the consciousness that made it. Therefore, we need to know what inspires our vitality, where the "gold" of our essential selves resides if we are to bring it forth. Our personalities seek power *over* life to provide us with immunity from sadness, depression, failure and hurt. Yet only through surrender do we grow and flourish. The power we seek is gained *through* experience not mastery of it.

In an ancient Chinese story, a master potter was attempting to develop a new glaze for his porcelain vases. Every day he tended the kilns to a white heat of precise temperature. Every day he experimented with the formula of his glaze in an exacting ritual to achieve the perfection he desired, yet without the unqualified success that he craved. After years in pursuit of this perfection, deciding that his meaningful life was now at an end, he walked calmly into the molten fire of the kiln and was consumed. When his assistants opened the kiln and removed the vases, they found the glaze on them to be the most exquisite they had ever seen. The master had become as one with his creation. In surrendering ourselves to experience and our essential growth we achieve the same. Alchemy requires base metal to be given up completely to its transformation if it is to be turned into gold.

AUTHENTICITY

What does your life say about you? If you were to meet yourself socially, what impression would you come away with? Would this be a person expressing their individuality, impressive because they are really LIVING their life, or would you find yourself instead confronted with someone shackled to social norms, frightened to change in case they might lose some of the flimsy stability that familiarity, conformity or status confer? Would this be a person who inspired you with the refreshing individuality of their life or someone frightened that either everything would change or worse still that nothing would?

There are many factors that can signify either imminence or state of mid life crisis. One of the most compelling common denominators though is very simply a reduction in authenticity. By this I mean that individuals in the grip of crisis have usually become less and less of their authentic selves. Their lives lack the generic creativity that is so naturally part of all of us. They blunt the uniqueness of their authenticity. So what do we mean by "authentic"?

My own summation is that people who seek individuation through expressing their own true values in both work and play, who are habitually whole and truthful to *being* themselves rather than *doing* what they feel they are required to do, can achieve their fullest potential. If they seek to do this creatively, honouring their true nature, they will blossom and transcend any difficulty through simply becoming more of themselves and finding a way to express it. Those men and women who express themselves fully and authentically in everything they are and do on a daily basis, without compromise, will live their lives creatively in the fullest sense of the word. In so doing they destine themselves for fulfilment. And as you would probably expect, complete fulfilment in a life that is lived with unconditional acceptance for ourselves is a recipe for just the happiness we seek.

Does this sound unrealistic? I do not in any way minimise the practical challenges that such an approach will present. This is an idealised and pure philosophy. And yet this is a practical book. We all live in the real world and that requires awareness of how it works.

How to apply your new self and re-integrate into the world in which you live is a very real need. However, your first step will be to stop measuring your success by the accepted parameters. Find a different set of guidelines by which to judge yourself.

From a Coaching perspective, this realisation that the tectonic plates of change are shifting, is usually a realisation that we are becoming aware, if not indeed actively preparing for a more pure expression of ourselves and our values. The self-actualisation that the philosopher Abraham Maslow demonstrates in his diagram on the next page is just the same as Jung's theory of self-individuation. The importance lies in the fact that it becomes an inescapable need in us. Whether it is a re-alignment to, or a discovery of new Values, this is an attempt to express our authenticity; our real selves.

One influential model that Maslow produced was his hierarchy of human needs. Abraham Maslow was a psychologist from the 1950's who developed a much more optimistic psychological perspective than had previously been the case. He did this by studying individuals who he considered mature, successful and fulfilled and wondered what would be necessary to bring this about in everybody as the Norm. His model can be applied to child development, to the personal growth of an individual or to the optimum business environment required to bring out the best in people. For our purposes, we can easily use it as a starting point for individuation. The broader issue of Needs is something that we will come to a little later. Certainly to imply that this model has all the answers is simplistic and wrong. Mid life transition as we can see already has too many subtle nuances and individual implications to contend with to suggest that. However, it is an important place to begin, if only to make sure that the foundations for the new structure are being dug deep enough. The final stage is an ongoing self-actualisation; the process of self-discovery and expression is not finite but continuous, and with your commitment will continue its expansion.

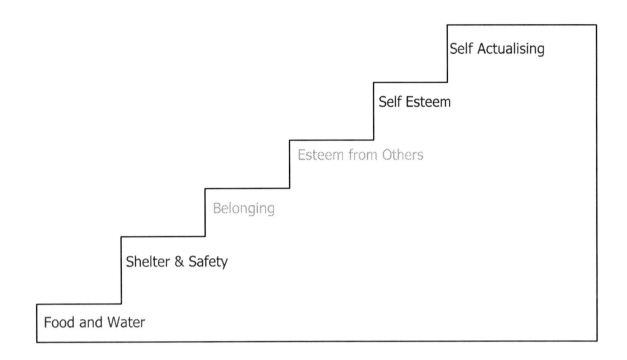

The Hierarchy Of Needs

(Adapted from Abraham Maslow)

If you view the above diagram as a staircase to an environment that will support the achievement of your fullest potential, then it is self-explanatory. Once we have the fundamental elements for survival and security, we can continue to climb the stairs to self-actualisation. The generalised template though, takes no account of the difference between individuals. That we all require these needs to be met in order for us to achieve self-actualisation is not in dispute. What it does not take account of are the individual's priorities. Put very simply: we all need to climb the staircase, but some of us will need the stairs to be in a different order. Also, once we have reached this stage of self-actualisation, we will need to implement a whole new raft of measures if the process is not to be derailed. The self-individuation process, if it is to be fulfilling, requires that we focus intently upon the expression of ourselves and of our generic creativity. The top step of Maslow's diagram is only the platform that we need to stand on in order to BE the person that we want to be, DOING what we want to do and thereby HAVING what we want to have.

NEEDS

In a Coaching context, and for the process of Transition to have a firm foundation, anyone that is making the journey of transition, will also derive great benefit from identifying their personal Needs and taking firm steps to having them met on a daily basis. The priority of personal needs cannot be emphasised enough. In getting your Needs met on a daily basis you establish a platform for having the rest of your life. Scrupulous attention has to be paid to this at all times.

"If you don't set a baseline standard for what you'll accept in life, you'll find it's easy to slip into behaviours and attitudes or a quality of life that's far below what you deserve."
- Anthony Robbins, author and performance expert

As with all successful prototypes, form follows function. Whatever the aesthetically pleasing shape and form of your present life structure, it may need to be taken back to its foundations and re-built if it is to survive the demands of the next couple of decades. And the chances are that if it is well built enough with a design that encompasses all of the requisite tolerances, stresses and strains, any future changes will be easily achieved. As any student of architecture knows: if you want to build something substantial, the first thing you do is start digging.

The first questions to be answered, therefore, are what job is the proposed structure being designed to accomplish and what environment will it have to provide. You are staring at a blank piece of paper here, with an opportunity to evaluate comprehensively what it is that you want. How do you want to BE...?

In answering this enormous question, it will help you to begin identifying your Needs.

As a pre-requisite for a healthy and sustained life through and after transition, your Needs will have to be met completely if you are to BE the person that you want to BE. We will come to the equally important subject of Values a little later, but for now simply imagine yourself as a vessel capable of holding all the potential for your true individual expression. When full to the brim, your vessel is complete. It is you in all your uniqueness, confidently and securely expressing your unique Values, living your life in a truly creative way, happy in the fulfillment that this brings you. Now imagine that your Needs are holes punched roughly in the skin of this perfect vessel. The liquid of your expression now leaks through the holes and instead of your vessel being full to the brim and perfect, you find yourself instead constantly engaged in trying to re-fill it. The effort and attention of this takes you away from personal expression and diverts you instead into a kind of daily subconscious crisis management. Instead OF BEING the person that you are here to be, you are DOING something that not only does not express you, but also takes you away from the very act of being able to. Some of these influences may be very subtle. Over time however, they diminish us. They dim our expression. They suck the vitality out of our souls.

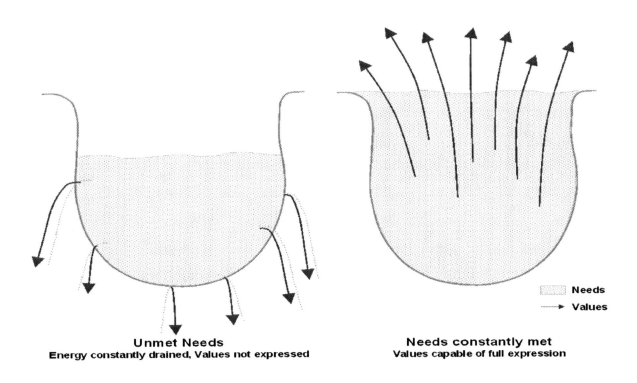

Unmet Needs
Energy constantly drained, Values not expressed

Needs constantly met
Values capable of full expression

Needs
Values

Read through the following list of words that are conveniently categorized under sub-headings and make a mark by any that resonate with you. You may experience quite strong emotional or physiological reactions to some of these. Take your time over this. Make it a reductive process of elimination to leave you with around ten words that in some way encapsulate your innermost Needs. The key to tracing the way back to a core Need is to identify the benefits for you when a specific Need is met. Ask yourself the question: "How does my life improve and what are the benefits for me when I have this Need met?" This will assist you in clarifying whether a particular word is the strongest expression of a core need or just a signpost on the road that takes you closer to it.

NEEDS

BE ACCEPTED	TO ACCOMPLISH	BE ACKNOWLEDGED
Approved	Achieve	Be worthy
Included	Fulfil	Be praised
Respected	Realise	Honoured
Permitted	Reach	Flattered
Popular	Profit	Complimented
Sanctioned	Attain	Be prized
Cool	Yield	Appreciated
Allowed	Consummate	Valued
Tolerated	Victory	Thanked

BE LOVED	BE RIGHT	BE CARED FOR
Liked	Correct	Get attention
Cherished	Not mistaken	Be helped
Esteemed	Honest	Cared about
Held fondly	Morally right	Be saved
Desired	Be deferred to	Attended to
Preferred	Be confirmed	Treasured
Relished	Advocated	Tenderness
Adored	Encouraged	Receive gifts
Touched	Understood	Embraced

CERTAINTY

Clarity

Accuracy

Assurance

Obviousness

Guarantees

Promises`

Commitments

Exactness

Precision

BE COMFORTABLE

Luxury

Opulence

Excess

Prosperity

Indulgence

Abundance

Not work

Taken care of

Served

TO COMMUNICATE

Be heard

Gossip

Tell stories

Make a point

Share

Talk

Be listened to

Comment

Informed

TO CONTROL

Dominate

Command

Restrain

Manage

Correct others

Be obeyed

Not ignored

Keep status quo

Restrict

BE NEEDED

Improve others

Be a critical link

Be useful

Be craved

Please others

Affect others

Need to give

Be important

Be material

DUTY

Obligated

Do the right thing

Follow

Obey

Have a task

Satisfy others

Prove self

Be devoted

Have a cause

BE FREE

Unrestricted

Privileged

Immune

Autonomous

Sovereign

Not obligated

Liberated

Self-reliant

Independent

HONESTY

Forthrightness

Uprightness

No lying

Sincerity

Loyalty

Frankness

Nothing withheld

No perpetrations

Tell all

ORDER

Perfection

Symmetry

Consistency

Sequential

Checklists

Unvarying

Rightness

Literalness

Regulated

PEACE	POWER	RECOGNITION
Quiet	Authority	Be noticed
Calmness	Capacity	Be remembered
Unity	Results	Be known for
Reconciliation	Omnipotence	Regarded well
Stillness	Strength	Get credit
Balance	Might	Acclaim
Agreements	Stamina	Heeded
Respite	Prerogative	Seen
Steadiness	Influence	Celebrated

SAFETY	WORK
Security	Career
Protected	Performance
Stable	Vocation
Fully informed	Press, push
Deliberate	Make it happen
Vigilant	A task
Cautious	Responsibility
Alert	Industriousness
Guarded	Be busy

Now, continue the elimination process to leave you with four Needs. It may help you to look for words that mean the same thing and then to find which one word accurately encapsulates the others. For example, to be "Not ignored" and "Heard" might both be accurately described by "Being Valued". Follow your intuition here and for the present, do not give any time to logical concerns over how these Needs can be met. Simply know that when they are, your life will have an unparalleled freedom that you do not presently enjoy. This freedom allows you to explore your authenticity. When you have reduced the list to four, enter the individual words on the chart on the following page and endorse each one by answering the questions there.

Need	Why this need is important to me	Who am I when this need is met?	Who am I when this need is not met?	How well is this need met at the moment?	Where is this need not met at the moment?	What changes would I have to make for this need to be met?

DESIGN A SYSTEM THAT ALLOWS YOUR NEEDS TO BE MET

The components of this system are very simple. Although it can be challenging to implement them, this becomes easier with practice. The components are:

- Establishing strong boundaries
- Reinforcing your boundaries
- Raising your Personal Standards

Boundaries

We need Boundaries in order to protect our lives fully. When we do this we can freely choose how we use our time and energy as well as interact healthily with others. A Boundary is a line of acceptable behaviour that may not be crossed. If you were to imagine that you lived in a castle defended by a moat, then the only way to enter your castle would be via the drawbridge. You and only you have control over who enters the castle and who does not, because it is your decision to lower the drawbridge that allows access. If you make it clear to others what kind of behaviour from them towards you will guarantee access and what behaviour will not, those that love and honour you will respect the parameters that you set out. If you say to others that being overly critical of you, making fun of you, shouting at you, belittling your ambitions and achievements, disrespecting your need for privacy, or any other behaviour that you find unacceptable will not be tolerated, with their acquiescence will come a new lightness around you.

For a lot of us, setting boundaries is an unfamiliar and challenging activity. We feel others may not love or accept us if we change in this way. We feel that such forthright requests may be interpreted as rudeness. Here is a model to help you with this. Practise setting boundaries using language that feels comfortable for you while at the same time making sure to incorporate the imperatives. It is important that you communicate your needs to others in a firm way that they will actually hear, while retaining a style that does not feel awkward.

Four Step Boundary Enforcement Model

1. <u>Inform the other party of what they are doing that does not support you.</u>

It is very important to adopt a neutral tone when informing others of what they may or may not do that affects you. Do not be confrontational because this is likely only to make the other person defensive and lead to an argument. Also make clear that it is not intended to be judgmental of them. It is a very simple statement of your Needs. So this first step in informing them has to be polite, although firm:

"Duncan are you aware that when you make jokes like that about me in front of other people that I find it very hurtful?"

If Duncan does know that his behaviour is hurtful, so is doing it deliberately, then you will need to find a way to avoid being in his company. He has none of your best interests at heart and probably needs for the status quo to be maintained in order to reinforce his own status and sense of security. If however, he says that he does not (and for now we will believe him), you have a platform for making a request that improves his thoughtless behaviour and removes your hurt.

2. <u>Request that they change their behaviour.</u>

Again be firm, but do not imply any judgment. Simply make a polite request for them not to do it again:

"I know that you may not be aware of how hurtful I find it. However, I want you to be more considerate of my feelings in the future and avoid making jokes about me in front of other people. Do you feel able to do that?"

Both stating the Need clearly and enlisting his support in meeting it is reinforced by his own assessment of realistic success. Whatever Duncan's response, you can now move confidently on to step 3.

3. State the consequences of continuing this behaviour.

"Duncan, I am sure that you will do your best to help me with this. If it happens again though, I will have to leave and find someone else to talk to. Do you understand?"

Whether he understands or not, the issue is that he knows now how important it is to you and you have asserted your reasons with clarity.

4. Carry out the consequences.

In order to enforce the importance of this to you, you must be rigorous in carrying out your proposed action. If you do not patrol the boundaries thoroughly no one will take you seriously and your self-esteem will drop as a result. Be kind, be firm, be rigorous.

As you can see, a boundary is an absolute limitation on what other people may say or do around you. Through taking this action, you protect yourself from other people's insensitive or controlling behaviour. Try not to be put off by the artificiality of the language and make sure that your phrasing is comfortable for you. The more you practise this and implement it as a necessary habit, the easier it will become. Remember, that your language and phrasing has to feel comfortable and natural to you. The examples here contain the imperatives or direct requests that need to be included, but modify them until you feel comfortable.

It is vitally important as well to make your boundaries extensive. When you do this, it limits any other behaviour that could possibly disturb you. When a boundary is inadequate, it limits extreme behaviours that would harm you, but may let through those subtle ones that could continue to cause you pain. For example, stating that people are not allowed to raise their voice to you will be an inadequate boundary if you are still hurt by sarcasm and subtle criticisms. If on the other hand you extend the boundary by stating that people are not allowed to diminish you in any way, you protect yourself more fully. This may eliminate certain people from your life and others may need to be reminded again by your enforcement of the steps above. However, the greater ease you experience with yourself and others will be an ample compensation.

Raise Your Personal Standards

Once you have established and reinforced your boundaries, make a huge conscious effort to raise your personal standards. These are the behaviours that define your integrity. They can range from the very obvious such as not stealing and telling the truth, to the less obvious such as being unconditionally constructive in how you communicate facts or criticism to another. Make sure that the Personal Standards you set are within your capabilities and not unattainable for you at the moment. As you take responsibility for yourself in this way and focus on having your Needs met, you will find it easy to gradually extend the range of ways that you can strengthen yourself.

Identify three high Personal Standards that you would enjoy upgrading. Write them on the chart and then list the three best ways that you can personally ensure that these remain at a high level.

Personal Standard	Step 1	Step 2	Step 3
1.			
2.			
3.			

Personal Standards Chart

Raising your Personal Standards is a subtle way to both increase your self-esteem and encourage others to treat you better. All of us receive greater respect and acknowledgement from others when we model the behaviour that we would like to receive. Changing an everyday habit such as deciding not to indulge in gossip or to be judgmental of others' behaviour, may prove challenging, but can harvest a quantum return for you. And like many of the exercises here it intensifies the focus on You and not peripheral issues. It may seem a small step, but it is worth it. Try it.

AN IMPORTANT DISTINCTION BETWEEN NEEDS AND MUSTS

Just as it is important to define a distinction between Needs and Values, there is an equally important distinction to make between an individual's personal Needs and the "Musts" that social influences impose upon us. If we return to Maslow's Hierarchy of Needs for a moment, we can illustrate this.

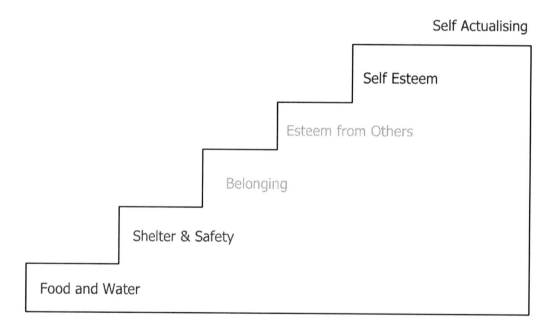

Working our way up the staircase again from the bottom, the basic needs for survival are obvious. Basic survival depends on food and water and having acquired them so are shelter and safety. What then of Belonging and the Esteem of Others? Whether these are our next priorities or not, as we ascend the staircase, they are essential. And they have certainly evolved as tribal necessities that over time have enabled us to further underpin our sense of security. But the basis for identifying "how" we belong or acquire the esteem of others has long since evolved from the tribal banding together that ensured safety in numbers and natural leadership. Now social influences decree that to ensure acceptance we "Must" have certain things – material rather than personal attributes that symbolise our success and achievement. Our "Must" levels increase. Consequently their satisfaction criteria move further out of reach. To have the esteem and acceptance of others and therefore happiness, we "must" have things that help us identify a satisfying social status – money, job, house, car, holiday destinations, even children. If aspiration of this kind is based on attainment that is permanently out of reach, then we become unsustainable. The staircase becomes a precipitous ascent as we focus on a hazy peak instead of consolidating where we are. High "Must" levels are simply damaging to the emotions and to your self-esteem. If you can reduce your attachments and bring your "Must" levels down, you will automatically increase your self-esteem. Focus instead on how simply and without support you can live your life. Concentrate on the really important aspects that demand no outside validation. As you can see from the staircase, having achieved this, the next level is the launching point for your self-actualisation.

Part of this personal re-evaluation for you is to strip away the artifice. Whatever badges of achievement or acquisition you feel make you acceptable, forget them. The only thing that other people truly respond to is passion. The only thing that will carry you through your day is fulfilment. If at the end of your life you are able to look back and highlight the important things, will it be the house you lived in or the personal joy you experienced there? Will it be the giddy corporate heights ascended to or the warm, grounded satisfaction experienced from a life lived in true passionate expression? Your decisions at this point may be the key to you closing this book now or to keep reading.

Still with us...? GOOD.

EXPRESSING AUTHENTICITY

A few years ago, the first series of "American Idol" a format TV programme that was to become hugely popular around the world was launched. The basic premise of the show was to discover new singing superstars. For participants, the attraction is obvious: anyone with raw singing talent and the charisma to carry that talent can be plucked from obscurity and become a star. The contestants receive huge publicity from appearing on the show week after week as the elimination process continues, so the promise of fame and riches is a real one. And for those for whom singing is a means of articulating their creative expression, this is a real opportunity to have a career that will allow this.

A couple of years ago, a girl called Fantasia Burrino was one of these hopefuls. It was obvious from the beginning that she had extraordinary talent. Her vocal range and depth was also blessed with immense power. More impressive though was the soul in her voice. The rigorous selection process requires that the final contestants have to venture way beyond their comfort zone and sing from every musical genre as each selection week passes, thereby exposing any vocal frailties or limitations that they might have. Yet, everything that Fantasia sang was extraordinary. She could just lose herself in the moment. From powerful renditions that transmitted megawatts of energy, to quiet soulful ballads, it was obvious that she was just <u>real</u>. With no ego to get in the way of her performance, she could be very present in the moment and just allow herself to BE. It was a special privilege to witness someone able to demonstrate this so completely.

As a returning winner in 2005, able to offer advice to the remaining 12 hopefuls, she said something that really stuck in my mind. She said: "Act ugly". Now that could have easily been misinterpreted. Not blessed with conventional good looks at all, Fantasia could have been showing self-deprecation and it is possible that to an extent she was. After all, this was a girl whose self introduction at the first audition included the words: "My hips are big, but my lips are bigger!" However, what I took from "Act ugly" was something more than that. For me it meant get out of your own way. It meant forget how you look, or how you think other people might think you look, or how you think performers are supposed to look – and just BE. Let your voice convey your message. Be real. Be yourself. Be authentic. Let yourself be what you were born to BE and then DO what you know you can do. The rest will follow. And for her it certainly did. The US public, confronted by the awesome authenticity of Fantasia Burrino voted overwhelmingly in the final weeks to make her a runaway winner. And what is impressive is that so long after that, nothing about her essential self as a performer has changed. She continues to "act ugly" and it is a privilege to watch.

So, to address the issue of "authenticity" squarely: How would your own authentic self be more fully expressed? What does not living an authentic life mean to you? Have you drawn any personal parallels from the descriptions so far? Answer these questions.

- What does living an authentic life mean to you?

- What parts of your life presently feel inauthentic?

- If you had a completely free choice, what would you do that felt creative?

- What fulfilling activities have you abandoned over time?

- What do you yearn for?

- How much of your day is spent in unwelcome routine?

- What does freedom mean to you?

IDENTIFY YOUR ROLES

Roles represent the key relationships you have with other people.

Roles represent your principal areas of responsibility in life.

Roles represent the areas in which you can make a contribution.

What are the roles you play in your life? Identify and list these, both in their obvious and simple forms, such as "Parent, Teacher, Husband, Sales Executive etc., as well as some of the less obvious choices – "Problem solver, Household mediator, Child Carer" etc. Don't forget to include 'MYSELF' as one of the roles.

Now ask yourself the question "Why?" to each one <u>5 times</u> and note down the answers. Spend some time contemplating what comes up for you. Remember, there can be no wrong answers and no right amount of information. Sometimes it takes a little while to even find the courage to address such questions honestly. This is an opportunity to begin designing a life that you feel would be worth living – whatever that is. It could involve just the smallest of shifts to re-orient your life more around your Values and to derive more fulfilment from the way that you live it. Or you could find yourself confronting major change. Either way, you can't be wrong for putting the time, thought and effort into confronting these questions. So take this opportunity to acknowledge what it really is that you want from your life.

Now list the people connected with each role, e.g. in your role as employer, the key people associated with that role would be your staff. As a parent, the key people would be your children. Finally, add a description of your ideal performance in each role - even if this is not the reality at the moment. For example, using the example of 'parent' you might write: '*I give my children unlimited love and support; I am always available to take them to important events; I make it safe for them to say anything to me; I encourage honest communication at all times.*'

Remember to use positive statements when describing your ideal performance in each role. Complete this exercise using the template set out below.

ROLE 1:

WHY: 1).

                2).

                3).

                4).

                5).

Key People:

Ideal Performance:

ROLE 2:

WHY: 1).

                2).

                3).

                4).

                5).

Key People:

Ideal Performance:

ROLE 3:

WHY: 1).

                2).

                3).

                4).

                5).

Key People:

Ideal Performance:

ROLE 4:

WHY: 1).

                2).

                3).

                4).

                5).

Key People:

Ideal Performance:

ROLE 5:

WHY: 1).

           2).

           3).

           4).

           5).

Key People:

Ideal Performance:

ROLE 6:

WHY: 1).

           2).

           3).

           4).

           5).

Key People:

Ideal Performance:

ROLE 7:

WHY: 1).

           2).

           3).

           4).

           5).

Key People:

Ideal Performance:

ROLE 8:

WHY: 1).

           2).

           3).

           4).

           5).

Key People:

Ideal Performance:

ROLE 9:

WHY: 1).

                 2).

                 3).

                 4).

                 5).

Key People:

Ideal Performance:

ROLE 10:

WHY: 1).

                 2).

                 3).

                 4).

                 5).

Key People:

Ideal Performance:

ROLE 11:

WHY: 1).

                 2).

                 3).

                 4).

                 5).

Key People:

Ideal Performance:

ROLE 12:

WHY: 1).

                 2).

                 3).

                 4).

                 5).

Key People:

Ideal Performance:

Roles and Goals

How much time are you spending in each role? Chart the percentage of time you currently spend in each of your roles. Is it enough or too much? How much time would you LIKE to be spending in each area? If you could wave a magic wand, how would you like these percentages to look? Mark the chart again - this time with percentages that relate to the amount of time you would ideally like to be devoting to each of your roles.

Example:

Now	Future version:
Parent - 25%	Parent - 20%
Work - 40%	Work - 30%
Spouse - 10%	Spouse – 15%
Self - 5%	Self – 15%
Community -20%	Community – 20%

This is an opportunity to be idealistic about exactly how you would like this aspect of your life to look. Unless you know, you can not begin to add the colour and clarity that the big picture of your life needs. I want for you to begin running towards your own unique "Big Picture", rather than running away from what you do not want or like about the way that you lead your life presently. You have to know what it is that you want before you can have it.

Now ask yourself these further questions. You will have other opportunities to ask the same questions again, or to add in more detail later, so just give the fullest answers that you are capable of now.

7 Defining Questions:

1)What do you Really, Really, Really, Really want?

ALLOW THE 4 REALLYS TO DEFINE YOUR ANSWER BY ENCOMPASSING :

a) What you desire

b) What you are willing to ask for

c) What you truly intend to create in your life.

d) What you are passionate about.

_____

2)Why do you want this?

_____

3)What is holding you back (or has held you back) from getting there?

_____

4)What will your life be like once you get there?

_____

5)What personal qualities would someone need to possess to effortlessly create the outcomes you desire?

_____

6)Now rate yourself from 1-10 on these qualities. (1 = LOW / 10 = HIGH)

_____

7)What are you willing to do to make this a reality?

_____

When you have answered these questions as fully as you can, move on. We will come back to them later.

FEAR AND ACCEPTANCE

A prime shaper of our burgeoning dissatisfaction as we move towards the mid life phase and the transition that we intuitively know beckons us, is our fear and dread of the unknown. Not least because we are beginning to realise that our present status no longer conforms to our idealised adolescent dreams. We begin, however unwillingly, to acknowledge the paradoxes that frame our lives: that as we reach our prime, we also realise there is an ending point to it all and that all our notions of the future need to be re-oriented around how much time there is left. To those of us still dug into muscular ideals of attainment, it is hard to accept the end of growing up and the start of growing old. Improved medical science may have increased our longevity, but business psychology seeks to shrink our work span. Corporations are not in the business of fostering your wisdom, just your gung ho appetite for success. Your experience in middle management is likely to keep you right there or promoted sideways if you are not already on a groomed fast track to the boardroom. And for those who lose either parents or friends of a similar age, there is the further chilling confrontation with their own mortality. So in the cold light of these realisations, it is difficult to perceive that held temptingly in the very jaws of this new danger is opportunity, the chance for no less than a re-birth; a second christening. In the full embrace of this opportunity new beginnings emerge. But the fears that accompany this realisation can be paralysing.

What do we normally do when lost in the dark? The man who has lived his life thus far as a masculine, seek no help, hunter gatherer is not likely to call for assistance or even to turn on the light. Rather he will stay busy, DOING more in order that the achievement of his tasks will help him to BE happy. Or perhaps he will continue to fill the void where the echoes of lost or unpursued authenticity might haunt him. Whether he admits it or not, he is trying to avoid Death. Pressing hard on the career accelerator, bedding younger women, playing harder, faster sports fills the space – for a while. However, sooner or later.....

"The first task of mid life is to give up all our real and imagined safety providers and stand naked and vulnerable in the World." - Gail Sheehey

In the first act of assuming real authority over ourselves, we confront the first of many fears: what if I can't stand on my own two feet? What if the structure of my life, however hateful does collapse? Such vulnerability is a strength, but it does not protect, it simply prepares. Like a mollusc that has shed its shell while it searches for a larger one to accommodate its growth, we are simply beginning the process. While unprotected, "...we will experience the wounding reminders of every unresolved, abandoned or unfinished aspect of our true identity." Where we have abandoned our authentic self, it will return to haunt us. The task in weathering this pain is simple: to return us to our true selves. Whatever private hell or depression this may plunge us into it has to be entered wholeheartedly. Avoidance will simply bring more of the same at a later date. As William Bridges observes in his book "Transitions":

"When the wheels spin in loose gravel, you need more weight."

A day at a time, a minute at a time, we absorb the painful realisation that through dismantling comes renewal.

What this amounts to is wilfully tearing up the structure that has supported you for the first half of your life. Not only that, but very often as a younger person you had identified just this structure as being able to support you for your *whole* life. It does not come easily now to accept that this might be an outmoded idea when your whole life is now founded on it! All that nature ever asks of us is to retain our adaptability and the ability to change. Our successful evolution is predicated on growth. What we now find ourselves coming to terms with is what that truly means.

William Bridges quite rightly makes a lot of modern man's inability to grasp the concept of growth, because we live in a mechanised age, where an article is delivered off the conveyor belt, in its finished and perfect state. Any future changes to this "perfection" are deemed something that requires repair. Your car does not evolve through its life. Any new sounds that it begins to make as it grows older are usually a sign of its approaching obsolescence. Why then would you as a man or woman, developing new and disturbing desires for self-expression, see these as anything other than something to ignore in the hope that they might go away. Such rattles and clunks will be an unwelcome sign of something not behaving as the manufacturer had intended;

something going wrong. Surely they are a frightening sign that what you have or believe is not enough. But you may not know what that is. Better to shut it out altogether. After all, becoming a sculptor will not pay the mortgage – will it…?

Our stability in the World is usually given credence by conforming to other peoples' view of it. We spend our lives culture and people pleasing. Therefore, in identifying that our spacecraft has brought us this far, we also acknowledge that now we have to jettison the main part of the craft and clamber into the unfamiliar cabin of the landing module. As we sit at the untried controls that will take us further on our journey, our sense of being alone is heightened by the knowledge that we are literally lost in space. The old craft cannot get us back and we have no guarantees that the new one can either.

Put very bluntly, as a reproductive species our only basic in-built need is to reproduce ourselves. As animals, no matter how far we feel that we have progressed in our sophistication, our DNA can still be reduced to this simple state. This requires therefore that we grow and thrive to an age where this can be achieved, a state easily reached for either men or women by the age of fifteen. Our only further requirement beyond this point, is to nurture our progeny to reproducing age. So by the age of 30 it is possible that we will have fulfilled those reproductive functions that Nature requires of us for perpetuation of our species and certainly by the age of 40 we are likely to be obsolete. But do we want it to end here? Absolutely not! We refuse to leave. We still pursue adolescent ideals of perfect love, great sex, unwaning strength, unravaged beauty, heroic achievement. We are totally unprepared for the rest of the life cycle. And our culture does nothing to support us in the understanding of our transition into eldership. We have no remaining traditions of the tribal culture, no rites of passage; nothing that honours our journey from one age to the next.

Those myriad established psychological precepts formulated over the ages in attempting to understand the mid life crisis, all point to it as being part of an evolutionary cycle. Even since Shakespeare's Seven Ages of Man in "As You Like It" we have been shown Erikson's three stages of Intimacy, Generativity and Integrity, Ortega y Gasset's Childhood, Adolescence, Initiation, Mastery and Old Age and Levinson's seven year cycle. A long time before these, back in 700 BC, we had the Greek poet Solon and his ten stages of life. Confucius espoused a theory of six stages, the Talmud gave us "Sayings Of The Father" and their very prescriptive fourteen stages, while the Hindu religion shows us a four stage journey of Student, Householder, Retirement and Devotional Spiritual Contemplation ("Sannyas"). And even this is not an exhaustive study.

Despite their many differences, what they all commonly demonstrate is that the middle years, if engaged with as a period for expansive individuation and growth, will reap a rich harvest of authentic self-expression and contentment.

Try telling that to the 40 year old man who for the past five years has had the sneaking suspicion that there is more to Life.

TOM

As a decent law student twenty years ago, Tom graduated with honours and a crystal clear idea of where he was going. The structure of hard work and competition that would yield reward, acknowledgement and above all bring benefit for people, suited his idealistic mind and held no fear for him. He would make a real difference and simultaneously bring himself the kind of material comfort his parents never had. During those zealous early years of little sleep and heavy workload his young exuberance powered through, until he began to experience pay off and the older partners in his firm saw the strength he brought to their organisation. They made him partner. He made his and the firm's name with a famous human rights victory and from that day, became the first port of call for any high profile David versus Goliath legal confrontation. His new wife was equally impressed with her newly found champion and happily put her own career on hold to bear and raise their three children. The expansion of the company, and the enrichment of its blue chip client base, led to its subsequent acquisition by a larger law firm, who saw an opportunity to buy the competition rather than lose business to it. However, this was a move that Tom was never entirely comfortable with, although the financial upside was too tempting for his partners, so he acquiesced rather

*than dissent and risk being outvoted anyway. With the corporate expansion though
came a move into the corporate market; he found himself rubbing shoulders with the
very people he had fought against so successfully for years. His cases moved into a
different realm and as the financial rewards escalated, his feelings of dislocation began
to grow. It felt a little better with the acquisition of a second home. He barely saw the
children growing up though. His wife Sally, bemoaning that she never saw Tom, began
to grow distant. He tried to explain that all of this was for them and that in five years,
not only could he retire and they could do whatever they wanted, but also that he was
not happy about it either. Could she not understand that? He could not just walk away
from what he had built up. His parents had put him through college so that he could get
to exactly where he was now. Sally pointed out that they had also wanted him to be
happy, but that went unheard. Also had he considered her needs? She was feeling a
desire to return to the work place and re-start her own career. The children were
becoming ever more self-sufficient and she needed an outlet. Tom's own growing inner
turmoil prevented him from hearing her. Any attempt to re-create a relationship with his
children was met with adolescent suspicion. Of course having missed those early
nurturing years, now that he yearned for intimacy, his children rejected it. Not cool.
Besides he was trying to have the lost, early times again; lack of familiarity meant that
he had no idea of how to connect with them now. He began to look outside his marriage
for comfort, deep down knowing that it would precipitate the inevitable. He had begun
an affair the year before anyway. The company of one younger woman and then
another did not have quite the rejuvenating effect he would have anticipated, but it took
his mind away from his unhappiness.*

What Tom does not know of course is that he is a working example of the well-worked
western theory that if he DOES these things, then he will HAVE these things, which will
mean that he will BE happy. For those of us with this ingrained ethos, it is difficult to see
a new way; especially when the re-frame I am suggesting implies such vulnerability.
Tom is struggling.

Let me give you the experience of a close friend. What I want to illustrate is how
counter-productive struggle can be and how *not* struggling can literally save your life.

Jane is a close friend of mine. Her birthday occurs the day after mine and historically we have often shared birthday experiences. One year on a significant birthday, we went on a surprise holiday to Zimbabwe, where we had an action-packed few days; bungee jumping off the Victoria Falls, land and river safaris, hedonism during a time when Zimbabwe was a paradise. One activity was to white water raft down a particularly dangerous stretch of the Zambezi. Although these activities are closely supervised, there is always an element of risk. Two early injuries to people in other boats was a sobering reminder of this. During the descent later in the day, our boat was flipped up by the convergence of two raging currents and Jane was tipped out. She then found herself doing what the locals call "downtime", where despite her efforts, the strength of the two opposing undercurrents literally held her under. Jane is one of the strongest swimmers I know, so I was shocked to find that when she eventually got back on the boat, she was ashen faced and working very hard to make light of the experience. When she recounted the experience to me later, she told me that she had found herself being thrown around under the water as though in a washing machine, and despite her strength as a swimmer, she was completely incapable of doing anything about it. This went on for about 15 seconds, at which point she surrendered. Realising that she could not battle with the water she let it take her where it wanted. Some instinct in her told her that struggling was the worst thing to do. Sure enough, almost immediately, the river spat her out again, a long way from our boat and we eventually hauled her in. I have never forgotten that experience, nor is the lesson lost on me that it teaches. Struggle is pointless. When life is not going your way, heed the definition between effort and struggle. Letting nature take its course may involve a lot of trust on your part, but the journey will be interesting and the subsequent outcomes more worthwhile.

As Hillary Clinton rightly points out, it takes a village to raise a child. Our Western move towards the nuclear family, dictated by many socio-economic criteria, has meant that we have moved away from the tribal society that previous generations espoused. We may not have had the community of extended family and village elders for a long time. We may not have been able to give our children the benefit of acquiring wisdom almost by osmosis as they moved around from one centre of influence to another. But we do have the advantage of our overview. If our children do not benefit from contact with all sections and stages of development within their immediate community, how can they possibly grow up to understand and prepare for the nature of transition in either their parents or themselves? Their experience, confined to the doctrinal teachings of their schoolteachers and the single paced nurturing (however loving) of their parents will yield a very narrow experience. They will typically have had minimal contact with adults outside the age range of their parents, no supervision by tribal elders or initiation masters, no contact with the concept of personal evolution and growth as something to be embraced. Instead, as referred to earlier, the mechanised nature and expectations of their lives will bring these transitional changes as a huge shock to them.

William Bridges quite rightly advocates against the transplanting of ritual to aid us in acknowledging these transitions, particularly the jolt at mid life. Tempting as it might be to re-invent such ritualised rites of passage, it is unlikely to do more than skim the cultural surface unless they hold huge personal resonance. They are not techniques for achieving the changes, but rather lenses to observe them through and magnify the experience. However, it is inescapable that the ritual as observed and accepted as part of tribal life can lead us to anticipate the journey and its colour. They underscore the constancy of change and the nature of renewal. Seasons bring with them the expectancy of the new. Planting and harvest are each accepted and welcomed for what they promise as well as deliver. And in any society that accepts the process of change as part of a natural cycle, that we are all part of, the concept of individual evolution can be embraced rather than feared. Personal growth is just such a process of change. Welcome it. Accept with gratitude the stage you have reached while looking forward to the next and with it the challenges it brings. If we could all re-align ourselves with this acceptance of the Natural Order, the "crisis" of mid life might well be replaced with a welcome for each stage of natural transition – and its gifts.

When we can reach this point of acceptance in ourselves and understand that there are more benefits than curses to be had from aligning ourselves to our new and beckoning persona, we can also accept the true nature of responsibility. Responsibility at its core is to ourselves. Any client that I have ever had, will have found themselves understanding the nature of being "self-ish"; looking after themselves first and better, in order that they can be a better spouse/partner/parent/employee/manager etc. Such self-care is important to your nascent individuation. However, the greatest self care inevitably begins with the pursuit of authenticity: exploration of our passion and engagement in our soul activity. The fear that accompanies this can be paralysing, for with passion and commitment we believe comes a loss of immunity and safety. But in demonstrating this to ourselves and to the outside world we affirm our true existence and purpose.

Furthermore, in demonstrating this acceptance we also begin the fulfilment of an obligation – to prepare ourselves for eldership. Within the tribe, even as a nuclear family, we have an obligation to pass on without judgement to those who follow. Those people prepared to engage wholeheartedly with their life process, learn from it, and see the fascinations not the frustrations of life, these are exactly the role models that the young tribe members can learn from and eventually turn to. There is no imperative here by the way. Living a life of service is the last thing we want to consider when grappling with a new desire to seek meaning in our lives, instead of demonstrating competence to the boss. You may find though on your journey that it becomes something you want to do more of and that in return your new philanthropy yields more than you would expect.

"Until one is committed, there is hesitancy, the chance to draw back, always ineffectiveness. Concerning all acts of initiative and creation, there is one elementary truth, the ignorance of which kills countless ideas and splendid plans: that the moment one definitely commits oneself, then Providence moves too. All sorts of things occur to help one that would never otherwise have occurred. A whole stream of events issues from the decision, raising in one's favour all manner of unforeseen incidents, meetings and material assistance which no man could have dreamed would have come his way. Whatever you can do or dream you can, begin it. Boldness has genius, power and magic in it. Begin it now!" - Goethe

PART 2

Navigating the Neutral Zone

"We cannot change anything until we accept it. Condemnation does not liberate, it oppresses."
- Carl Jung, psychologist and philosopher

The real voyage of discovery consists not in seeking new landscapes, but in having new eyes.
- Marcel Proust

One does not discover new lands without losing sight of the shore for a very long time.
- Andre Gide

****

No civilisation has lasted more than a few thousand years. Our society buries radioactive waste that will still be dangerous over a hundred thousand years from now. This is the delusion that psychologists call Magical Thinking. Somehow we believe that we will be exempt from the griefs and losses that have afflicted others and instead be protected. This will never be so. The same denial of our elemental energies may mean that over time, the pressurised reactor that we have created for ourselves begins to slowly leak. Those trapped and unexpressed energies will emerge and run our lives in unconscious ways. Or perhaps rather than a slow leakage, we will experience a Chernobyl like meltdown. Whatever the eventual outcome, it will have come as a result of not confronting our fears and vulnerabilities.

The Be, Do, Have philosophy and its intrinsic importance to re-orienting around our Values, requires that we re-inform ourselves in BEING the very person that we want to be; all very easy in theory and attractive as a concept. Just the idea of this might speak to our very soul as a chance to re-define ourselves in the world. It is after all an opportunity to forge ourselves in a new way that expresses us purely and with fulfilment in the time that we have left. But make no mistake: the forge can be a crucible. The theoretical process that we enjoy so much can be a practical re-birth in fire, lonely, deprived of familiar surroundings and a damning challenge to our commitment to self. There is rarely an easy road.

Whatever circumstances have brought you to this point, acceptance of the change is critical. The surrender that we discussed in Part 1 has to be yours alone. Instead of wielding power over experience, seek to gain power *through* experience – whatever the interim outcomes. To find the way, you have to be lost first. There is no immunity and no safety.

The characterising state of The Neutral Zone is the nothingness that accompanies it. Rather like embarking on a boat journey to cross a river where you cannot see the other side, it is easy to begin wondering during the journey if there actually *is* another side. When the "Doing" of getting ourselves across a specific river is replaced by the "Being" on a journey of an undefined passage, this can be very uncomfortable. You may well know that you have started, but in true western fashion you expect to know when to finish. Emptiness for us usually represents the absence of something and since you lack even the knowledge of what that "something" might be, there is no certainty of recognising the change when it happens. In legend and in sacred text there is an understanding of the quest or the ordeal through which the person endures to change from what he was to something renewed. We lack in our culture the gap period of isolation and contemplation that accompanies such ritualised rites of passage. We are not used to emptiness, silence, absence of stimulus, or any state of true solitude that provides the space for our inner growth. In a world where the car is either moving or stopped, we have no emotional understanding of the state where it does neither. We constantly seek the reassurance of definition, of opportunities actively searched for, conscious expansion of our options. Although we have already noted that the surrender required of us is not wholly passive and requires the vigilance to take action where necessary, this part of the journey needs a willingness to go deeper in rather than more expansively out. That will come later. When you are truly ready to make the new beginning, the opportunities will find you. Almost like a chance encounter on the road, the new you will meet the old you travelling in the opposite direction. Renewal is achieved through repair.

This new introspection need not be interpreted as pointless navel gazing. Neither is it obsessive and selfish behaviour. Reassure those close to you if necessary that this is time spent beneficially for everyone. Going off alone can actually be a selfless act. You do not have to be prepared to give your best until you discover who you are and what your best is. And when you have achieved that, you will be a better partner, parent, friend and family member for all concerned.

There is a need to be primed for action while passive. Rather like a gently coiled spring you are in a position to act as soon as necessary, but without the over-stressed tension of waiting. Since this is an open-ended period of reflection and adjustment, see how you might creatively challenge yourself to spend time in solitude. It is usual for people in transition to begin seeking solitude for reasons they cannot fathom. Silence and opportunity for contemplation beckon. Long solitary walks become not just attractive but a daily ritual. I had a client who spent the period around his 40th birthday camped alone on a remote Welsh hillside. Sitting up all night staring into the fire may not seem like a constructive activity, but for him it was a definitive part of his journey process. It typified his newly found desire to seek out a contemplative space and just Be. The answers to your life may not come as a blinding flash at such times, (although they sometimes do), but the opportunity for nurturing recovery and awakened awareness certainly will.

Whether you choose to take up Yoga and Meditation, or simply walk the dog for longer, practise T'ai Chi, start rowing, begin painting water colour landscapes or take up hill walking, the end you seek is time to think and reflect – even if to begin with you do neither. It is an opportunity for you to be with yourself. Leave your novel behind. Forget the newspapers. Reassure your friends and family. This is a time for you to begin your adjustment to BEING – whatever that means for now. And do not place yourself under additional stress for this to be an overnight metamorphosis. Your first task is to accept the lack of definition.

ENGAGEMENT

A definitive way to affirm this new decision can often come from an engagement with the nature of our purpose. Mythology down the ages has told colourful stories of a hero's struggle with the world and its many beasts to eventually emerge victorious. We have to look no further than say the tales of Odysseus, Beowulf or Oedipus to see the reflection of crisis in the mirror that we are holding. If you are willing to transpose yourself into that same hero's state; to see yourself as a hero or heroine pursuing their life purpose at all costs, like Beowulf ready to enter the lake and do battle with the mother of his nemesis, then through such courage and commitment you will taste victory.

Become used to the pattern of emptiness and the germination of the seed of your renewal taking place invisibly. This is something we are not used to in the Western world of "add water and mix". Those enlightened societies and cultures that designed rituals for our passages of transition did not do so through description. The depth of the experience could not be captured through simple explanation. Rather they conveyed their wisdom and insights dramatically through myth and heroic stories, thereby raising us to the same hero status for engaging with a purpose for our lives and a willingness to transform where necessary.

"Our life is not given to us – we did not give it to ourselves – but it is not given to us ready-made. It is not a thing whose being is fixed once and forever, but a task, something which has to be created – in short, a drama".

- Ortega y Gasset

So be a hero. Accept that you are on a mythical journey of your own that holds all the elements of danger, fear and those personal tests that will ultimately define you and go forward. If it helps you to see yourself somehow outside yourself and on a path to enlightenment and authenticity, then do so. Confront and engage.

BEOWULF

Since we have mentioned Beowulf, let him be a first example; the heroic myth that encompasses so much more than an epic folklore. The story of Beowulf is very simple. A 1,500 year old anonymous Old English morality tale, it is a story of descent into the waters of the unconscious. He is a warrior in the most masculine sense, yet his survival ultimately relies on a more profound, less tangible inner power.

Beowulf was a prince and a warrior. Hearing that Hrothgar, King of Denmark cannot defeat the diabolical and predatory swamp creature Grendel, he presents himself at court as the answer to his problems. Apparently at night after the feasting, a large green creature smeared with mud would emerge from the lake and entering the hall would tear Hrothgar's best warriors limb from limb before dragging their remains back to the swamp.

To us this may sound like the stuff of fairy tales, but it does nonetheless bear an uncomfortable resemblance to what happens to those of us who ignore our more generically creative urges. In the broad light of day at work, or during feasting and celebrations when we are being rewarded and applauded, all is fine. But alone in the small hours of the morning, when we feel defenceless and can not sleep, a huge green hand rises from the depths and drags us down to – what? Our ignored desires for self-expression? David Whyte describes it for us:

"To the part of us that gets its sense of identity from the position it occupies in the hierarchy and the car it drives, it comes to feel as if it is being torn limb from limb. Most successful consultants and corporate trainers if they take the creative urgencies of their work seriously, wake up in strange hotel rooms at regular intervals and see familiar trails of blood leading back to this timeless swamp".

Joseph Campbell used to say that if you do not come to know the deeper mythic resonances that make up your life, the mythic resonances will simply rise up and take you over. In other words if you do not live out your mythic journey consciously, the myth will simply live you against your will. What would you prefer: to engage with this process consciously or to be dragged into the swamp screaming?

Beowulf is welcomed by Hrothgar and that night in the great hall of Herot, he lies in wait for Grendel with his men. The creature arrives. In the ensuing fight Beowulf demonstrates all the courage he is renowned for and mortally wounds Grendel who staggers off to die. Beowulf is a hero. There is huge feasting and celebration as he is feted by Hrothgar. The bounty hunter has triumphed. It would seem that the problem has been solved in one swift action. But that night, as Beowulf and his men sleep in a different hall, something else comes from the swamp and wreaks carnage – Grendel's mother. It is not the beast that we must fear, but the thing that gave birth to it. How many individuals, perhaps including you have confronted a personal inner challenge and in believing that you have resolved it, realise instead that lurking behind it is something much more personally challenging and that you have dealt only with the iceberg's tip?

Hrothgar is bereft. His closest friend and confidant has been taken. Beowulf is visibly moved and realises that the nature of the battle has changed. This is now far more of a personal challenge. He decides he must go down into the lake where Grendel's mother lives to confront her. The parallels are obvious here. There comes a time when we have to take responsibility. No more blaming. Go down into the dark, uncharted waters of your personal lake and deal with the problem. Grendel's mother is our disowned, unexpressed "creative" side. To own his full potential, first Beowulf will have to confront it – however terrifying that might be.

In descending into our own personal dark lake, we are confronted by those same fears that can always haunt us. Fear of what we might discover about ourselves, fear of failure, of success, of what we may have to leave behind. The only certainty is that if we do not take the plunge, one day the monster will reach out and grab us anyway. And since our worst fears are irrational, we cannot find their resolution through reason.

So what does Beowulf do at this point? He arms himself with the helmet of the King and the mighty sword Hrunting. These are weapons that certainly give him courage, although as the story progresses, we realise that his power seems to have much more to do with *disarming*. Once he has leapt into the water clad in his chain mail and sunk to the bottom in pursuit of Grendel's mother, he realises that the great sword Hrunting is of no use to him in the pitch black and discards it along with the helmet. He is forced to wrestle unarmed with the she monster. Locked together they fight until Beowulf is exhausted, unable to overcome the vengeful creature. Finally, they tumble into the very den of her lair, where he sees glowing on the wall a strange and marvellous sword. He breaks the chain that holds it by its hilt and with a single blow kills Grendel's mother with its glowing blade.

What are the inferences that we can gather from this story? However well we arrange for our self-protection, the true steel lies within us. Neither the armour of the technology that we surround ourselves with, nor the status we occupy, will insulate us from the monster we have to tackle because it lies within. If we follow Beowulf's example, we can see that it is through divesting ourselves of these trappings, or at the very least refusing to rely on them, that we make ourselves vulnerable and therefore open to going forward. Navigating the Neutral Zone can be a long and lonely time spent in a dark, frightening place, but it is only by accepting this and consciously engaging that we grasp responsibility for ourselves and our futures. All of Beowulf's armour and weapons serve only to weigh him down. Ultimately his triumph comes through discarding them and relying instead on his own abilities and courage.

Beowulf's friends wait on the shore for a very long time for him to re-emerge. The sense is of a long vigil, the three days and nights that constitute an initiation. Jonah was in the belly of the whale for three days and nights, Gilgamesh was in the cave without food and water for the same period of time. It is the interminable time that lasts so much longer than we would choose. Yet only by refusing to give up and staying the course do we ever triumph. The darkest hour is before dawn.

As we go through our lives we get to know these dark phases. The break up of relationships, bereavement, loss; such are the elements of a rite of passage and they will test us beyond our experience. We question our luck, our sanity, our religion – anything that puts the problem outside of us or beyond our control. Yet only by engaging actively and accepting do we move forward. A client of mine mournfully joked once that he felt he had to reach up to touch bottom. That was just before the commissioning of his first book, the arrival of a new and meaningful relationship and achieving closure on his past damaging behaviours.

I do not mean to paint a too bleak or negative picture here. However, it is important to realise that this period spent in the wilderness for those of us who experience the rigours of mid life transition, is the most testing but necessary passage. Out of chaos comes order. Out of darkness comes light. By consciously committing to this process and all the rigours of the roughest voyage, you will be cast into calm waters. Like the story of Jane earlier, surrender leads to deliverance.

So to return to Beowulf, he emerges from the lake with the severed head of Grendel, a dramatic image. After killing his mother he has searched the cave and found his body. Yet the sword that he found and used to such devastating effect has dissolved away in Grendel's blood. Just as the enemy that frightened us now melts away, so does the means that we employ to defend ourselves. We can never boast of our mastery. It is evanescent. Whatever means we have discovered within ourselves, they are for our experience alone. You cannot wield the same sword in the world above. The inner mastery quietly informs the outer. It will take some patience on your part to establish your new World view and understand just how you have changed. In Part 3 you will have an opportunity to explore this deeply with help from the tools and questions there. Early clarification of this can begin with an assessment of which Values are important to you now. What are the aspects of yourself that you want to express from now on?

VALUES

We looked earlier at defining your personal Needs and addressing them. Once you have done this and have identified the ways that you can have your Needs met on a permanent basis, you can in turn begin defining your Values and the kind of life that will best honour you. Your Values are an expression of you at your core. Values are those things that you are naturally attracted to doing and being. When you are expressing your values you are most yourself and most fulfilled. Your life and business will proceed much more smoothly when aligned with your core values.

Take the time to think carefully about the following questions and answer them as honestly and as specifically as possible. Your answers will help you to determine those things that are of key importance in your life.

- If you were to do one thing in your professional life that would have the most impact, what would that one thing be?

- If you were to do one thing in your personal life that would have the most impact, what would that one thing be?

- What are the tangible and intangible things that you would most like to have in your life?

- What would you most like to do with your life?

- What kind of person would you most like to be?

DETERMINING YOUR KEY VALUES

Look back over your life and try to recall times when you felt completely yourself - when you felt alive, excited, fulfilled and full of natural energy. Was it when you used to draw and paint as a child? We are all generically creative, but perhaps you need to be literally so and express this as a value. Perhaps it was the time when you travelled to some exotic part of the world, or decided to take up hang-gliding or rock climbing? If so, then maybe one of your key values would be 'adventure'. Values are ideals. They are the things, experiences, qualities and principles that you would most like to have in your life and express you. Remember you are in pursuit of authenticity. Ignore the apparently illogical nature of some of your wilder inspirations. And avoid at all costs any urge to be self-discounting. There is no standard or rule that says you are not capable of doing something that you choose. The details will follow. Establish how you want to BE before you decide whether it is something that you can DO.

Be aware of your priorities? If one of your top priorities is spending time with your spouse and children then one of your key values might be 'family'. As you identify your values, it's a good idea to define them. By clarifying your values, they become more real to you. Also, your definition may be very different from someone else's. For example, to you, 'Professionalism' might mean 'delivering a consistently five-star service' whereas for someone else it might be 'always showing up on time for appointments.' When you write your personal definitions, be sure to use positive statements such as 'I am', 'I do', 'I will'.

On the following pages, you have an opportunity to identify your key values. Once you have done this you can list them along with clarifying statements for each one. As you do this though, hold one very important distinction in your mind. It is often easy to confuse the difference between Needs and Values. Check against this comparison table to be sure that a Value that you have selected is not a hidden Need!

Needs:	Values:	Needs & Values:
Needs come from a lack of something that nurtures our lives. WE ALL HAVE NEEDS. They are created by us in unwitting collusion with others and are easily satisfied when we learn to ask for what we want and how we want it. Not having our Needs met can really get in our way. One way of noticing that our Needs are not being met is when we find ourselves over-reacting to a situation or set of circumstances. If you find that you are becoming very upset about something and behaving in a way that you would prefer not to, look for an unmet Need.	Values come from abundance, authentic self-expression and freedom. They can only be expressed and explored fully when our Needs are fully met. This gives us the freedom to be unique and authentic. Values are what you give out to the world. They are all about your own personal pursuit of authenticity and what/how you can express it most effectively.	Your motivation to satisfy a Need comes from not wanting something to happen that you know will have an unwelcome effect on you. If your boundaries are low or weak, events and behaviour that are unacceptable to you will occur/recur. Confusion over what is a Need and what is a Value might come about when your motivation to do something is really to prove something to yourself or others. If this is the case look for a Need! When you do something because you want to – look for a Value! Something that prevents you from acting on your Values is a Need. As a general rule you will find that Values draw you and Needs drive you.

The Distinction between Needs and Values

When you can make clear distinctions, not only will you have greater clarity around the boundaries that you set personally, but also what it is about yourself that you are trying to express. You will find that when you lead a life that is focused exclusively on expressing your Values, you are less thrown off course by the day to day events of your life. Focusing on your Values and how to express them most effectively, gives you the purpose to concentrate more fully on your aims and ambitions. Values form the basis of how you approach your life. They affect your attitudes, beliefs, choices and behaviours.

Below is a list of words similarly laid out to the Needs process. Read them and choose carefully the 10 words that really resonate with you. Mark each one for reference. This selection process relies upon you assessing your response to each word and understanding the trigger for that response. Those words that really speak to you will bring about a strong reaction either emotionally or even physiologically. There is no right or wrong response. When you identify a word that is important, you will just know. Check carefully with the Needs/Values distinction chart on the previous page to ensure that what you have chosen is not a Need. If you feel it may be, go back to your Needs selection and cross-reference your choices there. Then come back to your Values.

VALUES

ADVENTURE	TO CATALYSE	TO DISCOVER	BEAUTY
Risk	Impact	Learn	Grace
The Unknown	Move forward	Detect	Refinement
Thrill	Touch	Perceive	Elegance
Danger	Turn on	Locate	Attractiveness
Speculation	Unstick others	Realise	Loveliness
Dare	Coach	Uncover	Radiance
Gamble	Spark	Discern	Magnificence
Endeavour	Encourage	Distinguish	Gloriousness
Quest	Influence	Observe	Taste
Experiment	Stimulate		
Exhilaration	Energise		

TO CREATE	TO CONTRIBUTE	TO FEEL	PLEASURE
Design	Serve	Emote	Have fun
Invent	Improve	To experience	Be hedonistic
Synthesise	Augment	Sense	Sex
Imagination	Assist	To glow	Sensual
Ingenuity	Endow	To feel good	Bliss
Originality	Strengthen	Be with	Be amused
Conceive	Facilitate	Energy flow	Be entertained
Plan	Minister to	In touch with	Play games
Build	Grant	Sensations	Sports
Perfect	Provide		
Assemble	Foster		
Inspire			

TO LEAD	TO RELATE	BE SENSITIVE	TO TEACH
Guide	Be connected	Tenderness	Educate
Inspire	Part of community	Touch	Instruct
Influence	Family	Perceive	Enlighten
Cause	To unite	Be present	Inform
Arouse	To nurture	Empathise	Prepare
Enrol	Be linked	Support	Edify
Reign	Be bonded	Show compassion	Prime
Govern	Be integrated with	Respond	Uplift
Rule	Be with	See	Explain
Persuade			
Encourage			
Model			

MASTERY	TO WIN	BE SPIRITUAL
Expert	Prevail	Be aware
Dominate field	Accomplish	Be accepting
Adept	Attain	Be awake
Superiority	Score	Relate with God
Primacy	Acquire	Devoting
Pre-eminence	Win over	Holy
Greatest	Triumph	Honouring
Best	Predominate	Be passionate
Outdo	Attract	Religious
Set standards		
Excellence		

Once you have completed your initial selection, group similar words together. This is so that you can reduce your choices still further down to a final four. Be very aware that it is your interpretation and perception of these words that count, not someone else's. When you have formed these groups of similar words, choose one from each group that has more resonance for you than the others and by this process of elimination reduce your choices to the four that are most important to you.

The next stage is to clarify for yourself what these Values mean to you and how best to honour them in your daily life. Using the table on the next page, take each Value in turn and give your answers to the questions there.

When you have completed the table on the next page, it is time to design your life so that it more truly reflects you.

Value	Why this Value is important to me	Who am I when I fully express this Value?	Who am I when I do not fully express this Value?	How well do I presently honour or express this Value in my current life?	Where in my current life am I not fully honouring or expressing this Value?	What changes am I willing to make to fully honour and express this Value?

72

EXPRESS YOUR VALUES IN A PROJECT

One way to maintain these new standards is to choose or design a project that expresses these values fully. In a way, it is a showcase for you. It is an opportunity to reinforce your authenticity and reflect the life that you lead now in a very tangible way. Go public. Decide on something that you will find really fun as well as fulfilling. This can be anything you choose. Do not select a project that you are not ready for, or that you feel you "should" be capable of. Rather make it something that enables you to play a little and have fun. Do it, not because you feel you ought to, but because you enjoy it.

Whatever it is that you choose to do - learning to sing "Happy Birthday" to your five-year old daughter or sliding down Mount Kilimanjaro on a tea tray - allow no constraints. Anything is possible to a willing and committed individual. Be bold if that feels necessary and certainly unleash your creative expression. This project can truly reflect you and the life that you want to lead. Make sure that however big or small the scale, that you do this.

When you have done it – celebrate! You will know exactly how.

ALIGNING WITH PURPOSE

The new idea that you have an opportunity to live a life of purpose "on purpose" may come as an overwhelming shock to some of you. The concept of creating a definition of your "Life Purpose" may sound like a huge responsibility! It may conjure connotations of worthiness or evangelical zeal. Or conversely you may become excited at the very notion. Whatever your response, if you can see this as a keystone in the foundations of the life that you want to create, it will encourage easier contemplation.

Any of us that has looked for existential meaning can take comfort from knowing that putting "Being" before "Doing" has to involve creating a purpose for your life. As a result, your future actions will not be random reactions to individual circumstance or based on old habitual responses. Instead you will live your life "on purpose" and "with purpose", going forward positively in pursuit of the outcomes that you seek. We will deal with the achievement of outcomes in greater detail when we look at Goal Setting.

However, for now ask yourself some fundamental questions. You may recognise some resonance from the 7 Defining questions that you answered earlier. If so, see what additional detail or refinement (if any) colours your responses:

- "What do I want from my life?"

- "Why do I want it?"

- "What will it serve in me by achieving this?"

- "Could this have beneficial implications for others as well as myself?"

- "If so, is this (newly) important to me? And why?"

Your time management, or specifically how you achieve what you want most effectively in the shortest time possible, is dictated by the strength of your purpose. When working with clients, as a coach I find sometimes, the only way to keep motivation high is to align them with a compelling sense of purpose about what it is that they seek and then establish a focused and rigorous method for achieving it in the most effective way. Before beginning this, review your answers to the questions above and see how congruent they are with the Values that emerged from the Values Assessment and also your personal ideals. As you make any amendments, these should reflect your highest and best Self, engaged in a life that expresses you authentically and without compromise. You have an opportunity to make a powerful statement here.

Even by answering the questions above you can see that the route to defining an individual's sense of purpose can take some time and creativity. I use a number of different methods to arrive at this. The process itself can be very absorbing for both client and Coach alike and you have begun to cover some of the routes to this already. However, to cut to the chase, let us achieve a definitive understanding first of all of what I mean by "Purpose". Gerald Nadler and Shozo Hibino do this very effectively when they outline the "Purpose Principle". The word 'purpose' has many connotations:

Utility: - The purpose of scissors is to cut things.
Intent: - His purpose was benign.
Mission: - The purpose of the company is to provide conditioned airflow.
Objective: - The purpose of the bazaar was to raise funds for school equipment.

If we understand fully these connotations of the word "Purpose", then we can create a hierarchy of purpose for everything we do. Thus, if a proposed course of action does not fall within the remit of our agenda, we have to question why we are doing it at all. If that sounds challenging, for the moment absorb the rest of this material. It will help you to identify what is useful and takes you closer to your goals and what keeps you stuck right where you are.

We endow our lives with meaning when we can identify a life purpose and we ensure that this will remain on track when we validate the purposes of any activity that supports its achievement. **Anything that does not promote this is simply a deflection and has to be dealt with either by someone else, or as of very secondary importance - or dispensed with.**

The greater our purposes, the more creative options we have for fulfilling them. This is the exciting part. The bigger our goals for ourselves, the more creative we can be in achieving them and the more rigorous we have to be in our time management in accomplishing this. So therefore, let us examine the implementation of a purpose hierarchy to support you. Once this is embedded, the logistics of time management become not just necessary, but compelling.

EXAMPLE OF LIVING ON PURPOSE

Adapted from *Breakthrough Thinking* by Gerald Nadler Ph.D & Shozo Hjibino Ph.D and *Intentional Creation* by Dr. Lloyd Thomas and Dr. Michael Anthony.

Consider the relatively minor problem of finding a missing bicycle key. You have purchased an expensive new bicycle and since this was to replace one that had been stolen, you have also bought a chain lock to secure it. Your problem arises when you have not formed a habit of carrying the key with you all times, so sometimes you mislay it. Whenever this happens, your immediate problem becomes to: "*find the missing key*"; not a particularly demanding or complex exercise.

However, if you were to say to yourself: "*What is my purpose in finding the key?*" then a series of ever more important purposes would begin to emerge that question the importance of each preceding purpose. For example, your initial purpose for spending time engaged in a search would be: "*Locate the missing key*". However, there are a number of purposes inherent here that vary in scope and importance.

- Secure the bicycle
- Get to work
- Have the key available at all times
- Use the bicycle
- Get exercise
- Keep track of the key
- Have transportation

Now see that the different purposes can be arranged in order according to the breadth of their scope. This would take into account their hierarchical importance, so clearly "*keeping track of the key*" has its own importance, but is not as compelling as "*have transportation*". If you can continually assign a larger purpose to an objective than presently exists, you will find yourself addressing what really needs to be done and why.

Through establishing a purpose that supercedes all precedents you will always move magnetically towards what is really important.

The greater your purposes, the more numerous and creative ways and purposes become apparent for fulfilling them. A truly meaningful life focuses on the largest purpose you can ideally and practically seek to fulfil. The greatest of course is your Personal Life Purpose. What might that be...?

Quietly, thoughtfully and with as much clarity as possible, describe the image of your Personal Life Purpose. What are you here to Be and Do? Make this picture as sensory-rich and detailed as you can. See, Feel, Hear, Taste, Touch the experience of living your life according to and achieving this. What is it like? Give your description sub-headings:

1. What do you want to create?

----

2. With or for whom do you want to create this?

----

3. Who do you want/need to Be in order to create this?

----

4. When do you want to create it?

----

5. Where do you want to create it?

----

6. Why do you want to create this? Make this last a vivid amalgam of your appreciation and joy specifically related to the actions and the outcomes of creating this. Imagine the benefits for yourself and others.

Finally, in reviewing your description, see how congruent it is with the Values that emerged from the Values Assessment and also your personal ideals. As you make any amendments, these should reflect your highest and best Self, engaged in a life that expresses you authentically and without compromise. This is an opportunity to make a powerful statement of your own purpose to reflect YOU as you want to BE.

If you have been able to give full answers to all of the questions so far, a clear sensory-rich image will be emerging. If not, and this is proving challenging, then go back to the 7 Defining Questions and work through them again. Combine this with re-visiting the Needs and Values processes to underpin what appears. Remember to trust what comes up, however radical it might seem. Above all, suspend those life and career paths of familiarity that are part of your journey so far. Trying to simply adapt or modify your present circumstances for the future may be inhibiting your creativity and preventing more expansive possibilities from emerging. If you are meant to continue with them, this will be apparent to you, as will the changes you need to make. But if there is any awkwardness or emotional tugging away from these established paths, any physiological reaction or feelings of strain at all, take note of this. Allow the part of you that knows the truth, your inner wisdom to guide you. Follow where it leads, resist the temptation to edit or censor and then reflect on the findings. If these give you an uplifting sensation of release accompanied by an equally strong dread of the radical change they imply, then your challenge is purely logistical. You have an opportunity to express yourself differently and be creative in the way that you do it. Take enthusiasm from what the achievement will bring you. If the time has come for change – embrace it. All that Nature ever asks of us is to be able to change according to our circumstances. Anything is possible to a committed individual. If you own your passion and your purpose, the rest will be details – challenging perhaps, but not without solutions.

So in identifying your Life Purpose, inevitably you will find that lots of subsidiary purposes begin to emerge that require reinforcement and accomplishment to project you towards actually LIVING your Life Purpose. You are building a bridge between where you are now and where you want to be. Emphatically this is Being before Doing.

You are on your way. Write your Life Purpose here and sign a pledge to honour your commitment to pursuing it and the fulfilment it brings:

My Life Purpose is:---

I commit to pursuing the accomplishment of my Life Purpose, in order that I may have a life of joy, fulfilment and satisfaction.

Signed:---------------------------------

TIME MANAGEMENT THROUGH REINFORCING PURPOSE

Put simply, our truly effective Time Management relies on us having a sense of priority around our daily activities. What is important and what is not.

This can be very simply reinforced by drawing a Pyramid of Purpose that illustrates the underlying foundation point for your beginning. So it would begin with "*find the key*" from our earlier bicycle example and take you all the way to the top of your pyramid with say "*have transportation to anywhere, anytime that I need it*" as its overall purpose. Simple enough.

This is a good everyday example and can be easily illustrated in the way that I have described. But if we were to use this for a more compelling life scenario that could reinforce your answers to the questions above, we could show this more effectively. Let us say that you are deciding to apply for a new job, so let's call it: Your decision to apply to the Project X Company

The most effective way to view this exercise is to begin at the base of your pyramid with your primary action and then to continually reinforce your purpose in deciding to do this by asking the question "*Why?*" As anyone who has dealt with a persistent child knows, the frustration of constantly answering the question "*Why?*" can only be balanced by the clarity that rational and constructive explanation brings.

So answering "Why?" to the first question of applying to Project X may be that instinctively (and never disregard first instinct), you know that a successful application will:

1). Give you the opportunity of a career that suits your skills. (A valid reason, but not a compelling one).

And moving one step up the pyramid, why is that....?

2). It has the potential to satisfy you creatively. (A more than valid reason for further investigation).

So far, so good. But *Why*...?

3). "Because Project X is an exciting new and cutting edge development that can bring real benefits to people world wide. There is real potential in this market to gain satisfaction from something exciting and new, while bringing benefit to others."

OK great. But *Why*...?

4). "Well, Project X will cross borders both geographically and culturally so this opens up so many more opportunities for us as the providers as well as the consumers whose lives will be improved by having it."

So *Why* would you want devote your time and energy to this?

5). "Because I can see that through bringing my skills and creativity to this project I can and would maximise the opportunities for both parties. Accessing those new markets for Project X will allow me in turn to derive tangible benefit and personal satisfaction."

Can you see that by adding layers of depth to the purpose of pursuing this goal you achieve two important things: clarity around the validity of your task and progressive endorsement of its importance. All you have to do is to continually ask yourself "Why?" If you can do this at least five times, it is likely that the task passes the litmus test of importance. If the example above related to a person whose purpose was to be of service to the global community in some way, the answers would have been very similar to those in the example. If they were applied to a person whose defined purpose was to explore their creativity in say working with animals, unless they had a global vision for this we would not have made it past question 2.

However, if we assume that our governing criteria are being satisfied because our purpose is clear, then these positive answers become a reference for continuing to build your pyramid and it should start to look something like this example. As you move closer to the top, it is obvious that there are mutual benefits and satisfactions to be had from pursuing an exciting purpose that could provide a lasting fulfillment. And it could become real simply by following through on the initial purpose of posting an application to a company.

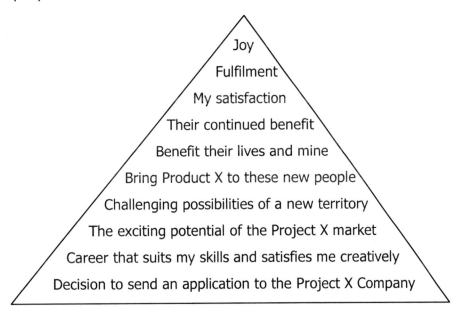

PYRAMID OF PURPOSE

This method of endorsing the motivation behind a specific activity can be applied to any scenario. Our earlier example of the bicycle key would be simple to engage with in this way. And knowing that *"having constant transportation to anywhere..."* would allow maximum freedom to pursue your Life Purpose goals validates it. Constant reinforcement of Purpose allows you to climb higher up your personal pyramid towards ever more simple and compelling reasons for being engaged in today's task. If there is no reason, then your first question to yourself is why you are engaged in it at all. This will inevitably enmesh itself in your Time Management effectiveness. The only questions that you ever need to ask yourself when considering the day ahead of you are:

- What is the best use of my time today?
- Will participation in this activity take me closer to the accomplishment of my purpose?
- If not, why not?

From the example that I have made up here, you can see that the intrinsic motivation behind the pursuit of this purpose is crystal clear. However, the method holds true for wholly extrinsically motivated pursuits as well. If your purpose were simply to make a lot of money and you identified an opportunity to do this, then the pyramid would be formed in the same way by identifying the greater financial purpose to each consecutive step all the way to the top.

Returning to our example though, the next step is to reinforce this with rigorous time management procedures.

The basis for these is very, very simple. Ask yourself the 3 questions above when even contemplating how the day ahead could be tackled. Personally, I prefer to plan the day before so as to have a structure in place and to hit the ground running. The day rarely goes as well if I start with a blank sheet. Also, this allows for planning weeks and months ahead with specific administration tasks like accounting and office management that the subsequent days automatically incorporate. However everybody is different and their most effective way of implementing principles varies. Whatever your preferences, as Ziz Ziglar would say:

"The main thing is to keep the main thing the main thing all the time."

Establish what your CORE ACTIVITY is (CA), delineate those other SECONDARY ACTIVITIES (SA) and make everything else DOMESTIC (DA). You may need to introduce one or more categories to recognise the particular requirements of your life. For example, if you are still working full time while you make the transition into your new way of being, the time spent on your Core Activity will adapt accordingly. However, the system works most effectively when the number of categories is kept to a minimum, so do not allow your working life to overshadow your intentions. Incorporate it and look at the ways to maximise time spent on your Core Activity.

Everyone's life has unique requirements, so for now I will use me as an example, with a random overview of how my time is currently spent:

Writing my book (and all associated publication activities) = CORE ACTIVITY

Coaching/client e-mails/research = CORE ACTIVITY

Practice marketing/biz building = CORE ACTIVITY

Research for my next book = SECONDARY ACTIVITY

Meetings/strategy and planning = SECONDARY ACTIVITY

Collecting the girls from school = DOMESTIC ACTIVITY

Building the barn in Devon = DOMESTIC ACTIVITY

Buying a new car = DOMESTIC ACTIVITY

Training for the Bristol half marathon = DOMESTIC ACTIVITY

The point I am trying to illustrate here is that whether you are popping to the Post Office for a stamp, or rather more demandingly buying a new house, the DOMESTIC activity always has the potential to easily swamp you. Some of those tasks can be not only time-consuming, but also have a strong pull on us emotionally. ALL three categories have to be accomplished to a satisfactory level for us to have an acceptable work/life balance and make progress within it. And yet, somehow, the temptation for DOMESTIC displacement activity to either replace or erode the time that we spend on the CORE ACTIVITY that is going to take us forward, can be enormous. Its incursions can be entirely disproportionate. Therefore, the only successful response is to be rigorous. And the only simple way to do this is to plan our day and make an objective assessment of how we are using the time. With clients I do this by agreeing what majority percentage of their working day they will spend engaged in their CORE ACTIVITY and then making sure that any SECONDARY and DOMESTIC activities are given a realistic importance by the lesser amount of time spent on them. The way to make it obvious is to colour code the different activities. You can do this with most PDA platforms and it is also possible within both Microsoft and Macintosh software depending on what you use.

So, if CA takes 70% of the allocated hours of the <u>working</u> day, (a desirable percentage that demonstrates your commitment), then the remaining 30% is allocated to SA and DA. This is focusing, because suddenly you have to be very effective indeed to accomplish everything. Knowing that marketing your new veterinary practice today is the only activity that will take you forward and reap the rewards you crave may be obvious. Nonetheless, the working day requires that as well as spending 70% of your time on it, you also have to pick up the kids from school, variously speak to the solicitor, buyer of your house and vendor of your new home, arrange for the removal men to begin packing and call the telephone company. The real challenge is can you accomplish the CA quota of your day without being swamped by the DA? So going back to the 3 questions I asked earlier:

- What is the best use of my time today?
- Will participation in this activity take me closer to the accomplishment of my purpose?
- If not, why not?

So, if CA is BLUE time, make sure that 70% of either your day or your week is BLUE. If your DA is PINK, the message will be pretty obvious to you if you look back over your day and week and find that BLUE is the least visible colour and that the colour of your universe is PINK! Realise that however overwhelming it might seem, UNLESS you prioritise the time allocated to your Core Activity NOW, there will <u>always</u> be a displacement activity of some proportion to erode the time that you could spend on it. After all, having achieved the momentous task of moving house, promising yourself that you would wait until you had done so to focus on building the client base of your practice, you will still have to unpack all those boxes. Then there are new schools to find for the kids, then getting to know your neighbours – you can't be rude and turn down an invitation to pop in for coffee, (can you....?)

Why so rigorous? Put bluntly, each of us has 168 hours to live every week. A 40 year old man with an average life expectancy of 75 therefore has 305,760 hours left. If ever there was an imperative to use your time well this is it. Your Time Management needs to be thoroughly effective in controlling the incursions of everyday urgent but not essential claims on your time. Be ruthless with those domestic matters that can distract you. Allocate and schedule time in a way that gives you a high percentage of time and effort dedicated only to the pursuit of your life purpose and all subsidiary purposes embedded in it. Delegate routine tasks to others, implement systems that support you, set high boundaries around your time and attention, focus on the achievements of the day and the week above everything else. The core activity of making constant progress towards achieving a life of fulfilment is paramount. If this sounds draconian, I promise you it is worth it and one day you will thank me!

So having run any activity that you engage in through the Pyramid of Purpose test to assess its validity for you spending your precious time on it, now you have to allocate this resource so that it is used most effectively. Spend a week or two keeping a strict log showing exactly how you use your time. At this stage, it will be interesting to see just *what* you spend your time doing and this exercise will begin to provide an indication of the patterns of your time management anyway. Whatever you do during the day, log it and at the end of the week, without any judgement at all note how long you spent on each activity then categorise as far as possible everything you have done into the CA, SA, DA categories. If there are any anomalies make a list of them to re-visit later.

Take a long look at everything you have logged and see how much of your working day is spent in the three different areas. Make a preliminary assessment of those domestic activities that could be either delegated or dispensed with. If it helps, give each activity a number from 1 to 10 going up in priority. Do not complicate this by subconsciously sub-categorising. Whatever the size of the task and emotional importance Domestic equals Domestic – no good or bad. Each activity has a number and if it scores less than

7 it has to be delegated or dumped. However challenging you might find this, for now complete the exercise. I should stress here that DA is the time during your identified "working day" where domestic activity intrudes. This does NOT include time spent with loved ones in an entirely constructive way, (although it does not mean putting off important tasks just because you are with them). Neither does it include time spent on your self care, which you take during your off or down time. Both of these are essential to a healthy work/life balance. The reduction of time spent on DA is designed to prevent you engaging in displacement activity that diverts you from your focus. Why go shopping when you can have it delivered? Why clean the house when you can pay someone to do it for you at a fraction of the time value that YOU are worth. Delegation of this kind will become a familiar term to you as you work hard at becoming this effective and see your purpose as more tangible as a result.

Now make notes of how you want to spend your time in your new idealised world. List the projects, proposed pursuits and all claims on your time then add them into the CA, SA and DA categories that you have created. Remember that some SA activities will eventually become CA activities. For example the book research - unless it is a primary concern - will only become a core activity when you begin writing it. However, the difference between the strategy planning that you do with your agent early on and the pivotal meetings that you have with your publisher demonstrate an obvious difference in priority. So be prepared for flux and change within your system and look forward to this.

Having finished the categorisation, you can now begin to input the information. Take care that CA is 70% of your working day to demonstrate the primacy of this and your commitment. SA and DA between them will comprise the other 30% and I would strongly recommend that SA is nearer 20% than 10%.

So using the chart below as a template, fill in the CA related tasks first. Be realistic and do not try to overload yourself. Setting yourself up to fail is not a great way to start. It will take some trial and error over time to understand how this system can best be adapted for you and what your capacities are. Treat it as an experiment and amend accordingly. See this as work in progress and whatever happens do not become despondent that it does not become a resounding success immediately. It will with your full commitment. Keep practising these methods and revising the way that you use your time until it works. The satisfaction and fulfilment that you are working towards are worth pursuing.

Below I have shown a way of doing this as a template. The important points to observe are:

- CA at 70% or above.
- SA at 20% or above.
- DA at 10% or less.

Note: I am aware that some of you may have life challenges that absolutely prohibit this. A single mother with one or more very young children and little practical support would quite rightly want to feed me this book a page at a time for suggesting this. As I make smug suggestions about utilising her time better, her reality may be a continuum of sleep deprivation and high maintenance of her wholly domestic life. *Finding* a further 70%, let alone using it effectively could be a very tall order in a life that is only borderline manageable. There are always extremes. My aim is simply to focus on achieving more of the life that you want and to exercise your creativity expansively in seeking solutions to improving your time management. This woman may find it more productive to plan and strategise for a time in the future when she CAN begin to implement these measures. Or she may find that she can make some gains today that she can gradually build on. There will always be somewhere that time can be utilised more effectively as long as there is a will to do this. I know of a woman who studied for her Law Degree in her bathroom. Once the children were fed and tucked up in bed, the only room where she could guarantee quiet and privacy for her studies was the bathroom, which she used for this purpose for three years! And this is the key. Whatever your circumstances, if you can commit to the constant effort of improvement, however small and incremental you are being progressive. Your goals move closer, the discipline of your effort sharpens your focus and the achievement of a life lived on purpose, with purpose for a purpose becomes real. Start now!

Below I have shown an example of a structure that you can work from as a template. Be free in your interpretation of this and adapt it to suit your means and needs. The main objective is to begin mapping your days and subsequently your weeks and months in a way that reflects the new priority that you are allocating to activities of purpose.

1. So to begin with, take a blank template of your working week as shown on the next page. I am basing this template on my own example for ease of demonstration, which begins at 7.00 after meditation has put me in a fit state to begin. Tailor your own version to suit your own routine. It is important that your new enthusiasm is not derailed at the first bend because your time management schedule cannot accommodate your everyday life!

2. The next phase as demonstrated is to block these out in colour to show where in the day you want to accomplish the different categories. This may take some radical re-framing at a later stage if the possibilities of this are proving challenging. However, for now remember that it is (and always will be) work in progress. Don't lose sight of that. If change will improve your system, then change it.

3. Having worked this out, now begin to input the tasks from your list that you associate with each category. Core Activity is paramount and displaces the importance of anything else. Where there is a clash, find a way to delegate a domestic task in order that you can use the time more productively on your Core Activity. How does it look.....?

1. Block out your working week.

Time	Mon	Tue	Wed	Thur	Fri	Sat	Sun
7							
8							
9							
10							
11							
12							
1							
2							
3							
4							
5							
Eve							
Notes							

2. Begin to allocate time to your CA, SA and DA categories. Check the percentages making changes as necessary.

Time	Mon	Tue	Wed	Thur	Fri	Sat	Sun
7							
8							
9							
10							
11							
12							
1							
2							
3							
4							
5							
Eve							
Notes							

3. Fill in your working copy and begin using it to check its manageability.

Time	Mon	Tue	Wed	Thur	Fri	Sat	Sun
7	Book	Clients	Book	Clients	Book	Research	
8							Exercise
9							
10	Clients		Clients				
11							
12							Off
1	Lunch/Domestic	Lunch/Domestic	Lunch/Domestic	Lunch/Domestic	Lunch		
2	Book	Book	Book	Outstanding Domestic	Off		
3							
4	Collect girls from school	Collect girls from school	Collect girls from school	Publisher's meeting			
5	Prep/Supper	Prep/Supper	Prep/Supper	Collect girls from school (late day)			
Eve 7 - 10	Research	Book	Book	Off			
Notes							

The important point to remember is that this is work in progress. It will not be perfect the first time and may take time to refine to meet your particular needs. Adapt and change as necessary so that it always supports you while achieving your primary aim – the most effective use of your time in the most important areas of your life.

JOURNALLING

Whether your perception is that you are even now in the midst of crisis, that the portentous black clouds of a storm are looming, or that it has already passed, it is important to maintain clarity on exactly how you are coping. Are there any recurrent themes having an impact on you?

What are the general feelings that you have about your life today? Begin to write about them. One essential aid to charting your present position is to keep a journal. No matter how painful it might be to write down the truth, take stock here. To keep an honest account of where you find yourself today and your prevailing thoughts is a major step towards recovery. Tell the truth. It does not sting as much as you think. Allow your thoughts to tumble out. Write without judgement or editing. Draw pictures if it helps. Let this become an account of you. If you let your mind roam freely, you will begin to discover yourself. If you can make this a daily discipline, one of the many that are now essential to you taking charge of the boat, you will find that a daily appointment with your journal will reduce the stranglehold of some everyday stresses. It may also yield glimpses of a yet to be charted course. You could find that amidst the rant or confusion, some half-formed answers begin to emerge. Early days perhaps, but instead of feeling that your life is slipping through your fingers like sand, it assumes a regenerative purpose. Whatever you do however, detach from the idea of linear progress. This is not a straight line to be drawn between where you are now and a future destination. It is a process of becoming. Just as the shell of a mollusc forms and hardens over time to give future protection, so will yours. But it takes discipline and it takes commitment to do whatever it takes for as long as it takes. Later on there will be realisations and you will be aware of encouraging change. Accept them. Acknowledge yourself warmly and continue. You are building a bridge between where you are now and where you would like to be. And just as a bridge builder goes back and forth over the same structure, day after day adding to its strength and shape, so will you.

The discipline of writing a journal also brings forth its own creativity. This is not designed to be a perfect book. On the contrary, this is the first step in encouraging loving acceptance of yourself and your life's imperfections. If your leanings are towards perfection, I would encourage you to lose them immediately by scribbling and scrawling from the beginning. If you seek a beautifully written account of your journey then you will miss the insights that sometimes come from aimless doodles. If you will not write down your thoughts as they come to you because you do not have the right pen to hand, you may lose the tantalising thread of realisation. When the clouds do part to reveal the pole star, you need to be ready. Carry your journal with you everywhere so that it becomes a dog-eared friend. Jot down every transient thought and fanciful idea. Truthfully and without sentiment acknowledge your state. Curse at the injustice of Life or contemplatively wonder at its implacability. You will find your course from now on much smoother if you view Life with fascination rather than frustration. Allow a picture to form that is you in the here and now - imperfect but willing to accept it.

If the storm is still raging around you, tossing you between hope and despair, take whatever shelter you can. However, unfair this period feels remember you are where you need to be. No amount of rant will change that. Detach from the idea of outcomes and assess your position using some of the tools available to you later. This reality check requires that you take a further evaluative look at your life circumstances and how you now fit into them. Look at the next diagram and see if you can plot your position. This is an extrapolation from the transition/trauma model that we used earlier. As you can see, it takes the form largely of a deep trench with sloping sides – easy to fall into, too deep to call for help, (therefore requiring you to save yourself), and challenging – but not impossible - to scramble out of. Where are you? Plot your position and begin to think about the implications.

Emotional Trauma Model

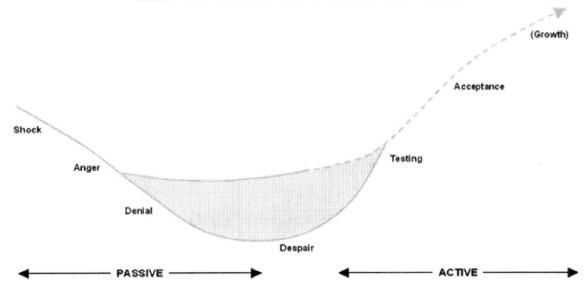

91

Wherever you feel you are on this path, acknowledge your position. Your commitment to the growth that is required of you is all that is necessary. The diagram above may allow you to plot your position, but here is where scientific analysis ends. Your journey depends on growth not linear progress. It is a journey of "becoming" rather than moving, as much to do with sculpting the elite athlete as training him. However, the process of self-individuation often comes at a price - for others as well as you.

Be mindful of the consequences for others during challenging times and resolve to reciprocate their support. The boats of those innocently following can often be capsized by the bow wave that results from your own self-motivated change in direction. Defying the tempering restraint of common sense or logic may be (and usually is) the only route to successful fulfilment. True success was never achieved by insuring against failure. However, we can make life very tough for others in our dauntless quest to seek out a new path. The unravelling of one life while pursuing another that has yet to be identified can have seismic implications as you test to extremes the love and support of those dearest to you. The magnetic pull of authentic living and the pursuit of increased generic creativity can lead to irrational actions and painful consequences, for a time at least. Be mindful.

EXAMPLE

This man learns his lessons very hard. His earlier "Catch 30" transition had led to the kind of cataclysmic event that just arrives. He could make no preparation for its arrival – it visited without appointment. A dispute over production standards at his high profile media workplace led to the entire work force voting to strike. Clever divide and rule tactics by the management led to a long running, acrimonious dispute designed to break the union's power. Three months on, he went on holiday to think about it. On a sun drenched beach in the South of Mexico, away from the pervasive rising damp of English weather and company politics, he decided to resign from his highly paid job, reasoning that whatever the outcome the working environment he had enjoyed so much would never be the same. He would go a different way.

Just as buses always come in threes, this episode followed not long after the end of a long-term relationship. He had been drawn into the orbit of someone he found more vibrant and the promise of an excitement he felt he deserved. The fall out from this was very painful to others as well as to him, but the price was worth paying he reasoned in return for the longer term portents of his future. Portents can be misread. Soon the new relationship was foundering, not helped by the tremendous strain he was under and his lack of emotional maturity. Events and people would be demanding of him. Much was expected that he could not provide.

His desire for excitement and feeling experience may have been unfocused, but for all that it burned brightly. He thought he wanted to be famous, to have the acknowledgement of the world. After all, he was special and different – wasn't he? He did not quite know what he wanted, or how to demonstrate this, but he knew he wasn't on the radar. What was less obvious was that he was having a breakdown. He began to remove himself emotionally from the world. Its real nurturing vitality denied him by the adrenalised existence that he craved and took for real living. The carapace that he inhabited allowed the world's voice to be transmitted to him only as blunt, dull echoes. He needed experience to mask his pain and make him feel ALIVE, show that he was brave and bold when he felt so small. Decadent hedonism was his fix. The Cresta Run, Skydiving (an experience that really DID nearly kill him), running marathons, driving very fast cars all failed to deliver the right …..what was it exactly? Not knowing was the basis for his life being conducted with such fractional tolerances. One night his alcohol-fuelled need to just feel something caused him to run at high speed endlessly round and round the narrow parapet of a top floor apartment, dizzy with the height of it, to see if he could scare himself. And still he felt nothing. The unravelling was gathering momentum.

And so it continued. The relationship finished in a brief blaze of press publicity, thereby granting him the fame he thought he wanted, just not quite in the form he would have anticipated, and the aftershocks were unpleasant. Debt laden and lonely, he shrank from daring to dare. It took a while before he could begin to explore how to go forward.

And yet go forward he did, armed with a new regime of purer obsessions to anchor him to the earth. Tai chi, meditation, strict vegetarianism, self-help manuals, New Age philosophy all formed the foundation of a calmer existence. He was a little irritating to those close to him and had more than a suspicion of the evangelist in his espousal of this as the New Way. Undeniably though he was growing happier with his own company, more accepting of the world - even if he still did not know what his place was in it.

And then he met someone - young, beautiful, vibrant, accomplished, unique - and fell passionately in love with her. It was an affirming miracle, a reflection of cosmic generosity for his surrender. She moved in the next day. Although the first few years saw occasional tempestuous rows, they simply mirrored an enormous passion and love. And he began imperceptibly to grow. The suffocating fear that he might disappear which accompanied the birth of both their daughters, instead abated over time to reveal to him the incredible gift of his own unconditional love and theirs. He was constantly amazed how much he learned just by being with them. And by how much he craved their company and energy as nourishment. Cocooned in this small tribe of girls, life was undeniably good.

This ease was mirrored on the outside in his professional life. He had a flourishing freelance career in TV and Feature Films, a growing reputation and consistent demand for his services. Yet below the surface there was a grumbling dissatisfaction. He was not completely happy. In fact, he found his dissatisfaction increasing in direct proportion to the size of the projects he was working on. Which did not make sense because the only measure he had of his own value and success WAS the size, (for which read importance), of the project he was currently engaged in. The paradox of this was unsettling. The bigger the film and the more tens of millions being spent on making it, the less happy he became. He began to experience disillusion about the lack of importance attached to the film itself, compared with say its demographic profile, or its positioning in the market for potential merchandising. Casting would be based on trade-

offs against internal investment into the film or future deals, instead of an actor's suitability for the part. Commerce grossly outweighed culture and creativity.

His own role, though powerful, lacked enough creative input or ultimate control to satisfy him and certainly could not insulate him sufficiently from the shallowness that he found so pervasively discomfiting. He was neither in a position to make meaningful creative decisions, nor change things, nor even to have fun any more. Ambition and desire for greater creative fulfilment, (and particularly lots more money), eventually prompted him to dismantle his career and concentrate instead on producing his own film projects. With almost no warning and certainly no safety net, he set up in partnership with an ambitious colleague to do just that.

Over three years, a business model developed to attract City investment into making quality feature films that were geared to both the European and US market began to work. He and his partner believed they had found a way to satisfy the remit of making quality films without being tied to the usual ransom of studio financing – it was brilliant. Private investment came in and the hard work began to pay off. The long awaited rewards for their three years of hard work were now visible on the horizon. However, they had been three very hard years. Initial optimism and belief had been chipped away at by many false dawns, broken promises and financial insecurity over paying themselves and keeping the company afloat. A wealthy friend who supported them in their venture and had promised a significant financial investment continually delayed committing the funds. Projects that had been commissioned and developed on the basis of this investment were constantly held up as a result. Important relationships with writers soured and deteriorated as they went unpaid and initial goodwill was traded on one time too many. Their company reputation in the industry also began to suffer. So although rewards were in sight, there were still hurdles to get over.

Relations between the two partners deteriorated to an all time low. Their earlier honest communication had all but disappeared. "Our friend" became unbearably controlling in direct proportion to his growing insecurities. Unable to take responsibility for his circumstances, he needed to have someone to blame. And so he focused conveniently on his partner, trying to control the way in which he operated and undermining the indomitable belief that he had previously admired so much and which he knew was essential to future success. He became negative and dark around the office, frightened that it might all come to nothing; scared that in his own as well as the eyes of his friends and family he would be perceived as a failure; terrified that having put his whole family's security on the line and mortgaged them beyond redemption that the whole edifice would come crashing down. Which it did.

His partner finally had enough and shut him out. Exploiting a temporary loophole in their partnership agreement, he took the rights to all the projects they had developed and to all future royalties. He made a private arrangement with their primary investor and moved all company assets into an offshore company. Despite the appalling disloyalty and malpractice of this, he was probably just surviving; taking the only way out that would allow him to live freely. "Our friend" might have recognised this. It was exactly what he had done when he left his last relationship. One day he realised he could not take it any more and that was it – he left, never to return. Survival. Such thoughts though were far from his mind. His only preoccupation now was not his personal safety, but that of a small tribe of girls. They were all about to drown in a sea of personal debt. He had broken his faithful promise that this would never happen; that they would never have to face this. He had committed the cardinal sin of failing to take care of those who adored him. He had failed himself. They thought he was a hero and he had turned out to be a loser. This was the cosmic collapse of a real Mid Life Crisis. What to do?

He checked his Life Assurance and contemplated suicide, reasoning the financial settlement as one obvious solution. He made arrangements to sell their house (an unavoidable decision). Weeks and months passed in a daze. All reflection and contemplation yielded no answers. He was battling in a whirlpool of fear and uncertainty, unable to find a way out. His anxiety and lack of confidence precluded him from taking any action at all: the paralysis of analysis. How could he rescue his family if he could not even rescue himself? While weathering his partner's occasional and very justifiable outbursts of anger, he found that he still had no answers. Had he done this on purpose? At some level was this all a magnificent act of self-sabotage?

And then they had a near fatal car crash. Miraculously, they all survived - he still does not know how. But as he stood on that sunlit freezing afternoon, engaged in the event but somehow detached from it, the overwhelming feeling was only that he was with the most important people in his life. And that he loved them and that he wanted to live and be with them and that nothing could be worse than being denied that opportunity and that while he brought up his girls to need no one, they needed HIM now. They needed care and they needed leadership and he was the best person to provide that. It was life altering. Ashen-faced friends fighting their way through a dozen fire engines, ambulances and police cars to be confronted with the wreckage and carnage were amazed to find him alive in the middle of it and calm. Everyone was safe. Could they take them somewhere warm please? He had to deal with the emergency services and the police.

That was four years ago and "our friend" calmly dealing with the emergency services was Me. This book is a part of that decision to go forward and demonstrate leadership. Part of my life purpose, as well as the purpose of this book is to pass on what I learn in order that I bring benefit to the greatest number of people possible. Being a Coach allows me that. Since becoming a Coach I have not looked back, other than to seek greater clarity on how I arrived at this place and how I can use this experience for good. Herein lies the generic creativity that is so fundamentally important to all of us and which informs the Being that precedes and supercedes Doing. It is a daily source of satisfaction to me now that my life allows me to be more creative than I have ever been and clearly my work has more impact on people's lives than any film I have seen or worked on. The progress and achievements of my clients are a source of quiet delight for me. I live a life now that I feel is worth living. I can look in the mirror every day and genuinely say that what I do has integrity and meaning and benefits others. This has been a long time coming and the way was not always clear, but I hope you can see it was worth the journey.

At whatever point you now find yourself, however lonely and uncomfortable you may feel, even if you are in the midst of confusion, hopefully one thing is very clear - your life is not over. Standing as you do, half way up the mountain, you have an irresistible opportunity to re-evaluate your route to the summit and the equipment that you will need to take you there. You stand in the same place as Mother Theresa, Gandhi, Cervantes, Walt Whitman to name but a very few who found their true selves and meaningful vocation only after a process of midlife transition. US President Abraham Lincoln's rise to prominence did not begin until his late 30's, when a midlife transition hallmarked by depression, an unhappy marriage and an unsuccessful career suddenly changed him into a man with a purpose for fulfilment. Eleanor Roosevelt had the most attritional of journeys when at around age 35 she discovered that her husband was having an affair with her best friend. Her own self-individuation in transcending this devastating discovery led to her overcoming intense shyness and self-doubt and was the key to her metamorphosis into the renowned public figure and champion that we recognise now. Most importantly for her, it forced her to make the choice to live her life outside the shadow of her husband the US President. She pursued self-individuation and meaning in her life. You now stand at the same doorway. With the smallest of pushes from you the door will open.

Your opportunity here is to identify the kind of life that you want to have with all its concomitant elements for potential satisfaction, fulfilment and as a result, long-term happiness. We can all of us experience a life of mediocrity and compromise. But is that *all* you want? With total commitment to your future and the full realisation of your personal potential, you will go forward from here. Half of your life may be behind you, but the other half, full of rich possibilities for your fulfilment and satisfaction, lies ahead of you, tantalising and glittering with potential. Like a path strewn with diamonds it is waiting for you to take the first step.

RESPONSIBILITY

One of the single most important decisions you can make to navigate the Neutral Zone successfully, is to take responsibility. Responsibility on its own comes at a cost. It is not merely the notion of accepting stewardship of a particular task. This is full and complete responsibility for yourself and everything that involves you. It is time to tell the truth. Where are you? What brought you here? Are you fully committed to a new beginning and the realisation of your own personal potential? Whatever the circumstances, take full responsibility for your part, be honest about the present and respond rather than react. Seek solutions. Commit to going forward and to becoming the person you need to be in order to inhabit the future you want to have. Does self-actualisation with all its promise of individual expression pull and excite you? If the answer is a "Yes" that makes you shake physically, turns your stomach over and leaves you slightly short of breath, then you are also ready to take responsibility.

Whatever the specific circumstances of the crash might be - own up. We all know intuitively our reason for arriving at this place: self-abandonment. At some stage, at some level you abandoned your creative, natural self. Parental conditioning, materialistic lures, career progression traps or any other reason from a long and detailed list. They brought you here. Can you assume ultimate responsibility for these events and accept them as both integral and necessary catalysts in the forging of your growth? Even if your personal circumstances as a child were the most forlorn in the world with no perceptible choices at all about the passage of your life to this point, take responsibility. This is your journey. Whatever beliefs about karma, fate, luck, privilege or destiny may have informed your thinking to this point, it is time to suspend them. Everything that you do as well as everything that happens to you from now on is YOUR responsibility. If you take responsibility for even the train being late, or the weather turning bad, then guess what? You can also take responsibility for all the good things that happen to you. Fate always needs your help. It's personal responsibility. Delight in this. It is empowering. There is literally no person, thing or event that stands in your way. You have power over everything that now happens in your life and no one else can be blamed for you not achieving it. You will no longer blame your parents for forcing you into a hateful career, or the lack of opportunities afforded by your childhood or the difficulties inherent in maintaining your family's lifestyle while trying to pursue new directions. You are the captain of this ship, in sole charge of its course – and where there is commitment to expressing your true creative self and exploring its potential there WILL be a way.

FORGIVENESS

With this taking up of the reins there also comes a need for forgiveness. This is essential. Taking control in this way makes you a big person. You now have a tremendous opportunity to forgive everyone in your life (including yourself) for past actions and move on. All that has happened to you so far has been essential to your growth. Everything that has occurred is an integral part of an intricate pattern designed to force your arrival at this point of decision. Events brought you here, however painfully and demand that you step up to the challenge. Without your past, you would not be demonstrating the commitment already of reading this book and making a decision to have more of the life that you want. As an extension of the responsibility you have now accepted, acknowledge your part in the circumstances that have delivered you here and wholeheartedly forgive those other people involved. They are on their own path. Their actions will bring them some other outcomes at some other time and you may or may not be present to witness that. But for now, your forgiveness does two things: it allows you to assume empowering responsibility over your present life circumstances and removes you from the negative energy of a blame and regret culture. If you find it challenging to separate yourself from the events and people of your past in this way, then when reviewing them, try to behave like a dog with a favourite bone. Every now and again you can dig it up throw it around and see how you feel about it. You can play with it, gnaw at it and even growl at it. And then when you are finished you can bury it again. The pattern that is likely to emerge over time is of fewer visits to the burial site as you gain momentum and perspective. And it is important to make a distinction here between the deep, deep burial of nuclear waste that will come back to haunt us and a coping strategy that allows for your clarity of purpose to take form. You may dig back into the past from time to time to lay old ghosts and achieve closure. Meanwhile, the focus is on the present and expansion into a planned future, without the spectre of past events obscuring the view.

I hope that by now at least you are identifying with your state. All the defining hallmarks demonstrate one comforting fact: you are not alone. However, challenging your journey so far, this path has been trodden before by so many other men and women that you can at least derive some comfort. The place where you stand today demands your acceptance. You are where you need to be.

Because we have no formalised rite of passage rituals that would place this state of our evolution into an accepted tribal context, we are presented with an irrefutable challenge. There is no expectation for us at a certain age to become a forest dweller, nor to go through ceremonies that require us to fight lions or leave us bearing physical scars. Instead, we go around in ever tighter circles aware of a growing malaise that we do not want to confront until inescapably we have only one choice: change.

This change will involve a radical re-defining of the structure that supports your life. Such change can only take place when the core of the challenge has been confronted, identified and marked for priority re-assessment. It has to be tackled from the inside out. There is no point in trying to re-arrange the deck chairs on the Titanic. You need to design a new boat. Ask Toby...

TOBY

Toby is 40. A Creative/Restorative client whose media working life on the glossy surface up until this point has concealed a snowballing existence of addictive behaviour, mainly around sex and alcohol, that has brought him to a crunching halt. His marriage is over. Any future relationship with his children will have to be founded on consistent efforts of demonstrable commitment if he is to share at all in his future parenting. His self-esteem is at rock bottom and he is very scared

Having entered a 12 step recovery programme for his sex addiction and having given up drinking as well since it is easy fuel for his acting out, he has turned to me for help with everything else. However although he has wonderful creative ability as a writer and finds this to be a perfect conduit for his self-expression, the breathtaking imagination that produces such vivid children's escapism is matched by an equally staggering capacity for self-sabotage. While one day might be heaven and yield beautiful, haunting narrative capable of transporting a child's imagination to exotic realms, the next could be hell as he fights powerlessly to escape a prison of guilt, shame and self-obsession. Inside his head, days spent in dreamy flow can be just as easily transformed into a spiky battlefield where his demons fight for supremacy.

Life has become very unmanageable. Although Toby has already begun to take responsibility for his circumstances, progress is still very slow. With freelance employment options very much in decline, Toby's world is delineated by spiralling debt, fear around acting out, guilt and shame for his past actions, low self-worth started by his parents and not helped by referential endorsement. He constantly seeks validation for his circumstances and status by comparing himself with others; a guaranteed route back into the vortex of shame as he concludes that everyone is having a great life but him. He is dragging along the bottom in the early stages of recovery where the anchor still seeks solid purchase to affix itself. And in the middle of this he is still trying to work and shine in the dysfunctional media world in order to remain financially afloat, when what he wants to do most is to express himself through his writing. Where to start....

When Toby and I began working together, we focused on two main areas: his very apparent need for self-expression through writing and the general area of manageability that would allow him to accomplish this. Since he had already identified the form that could express his creativity, we worked on simplifying his life in all areas, in order that he could have the space to achieve it. Goals were set that were designed to specifically further his progress, both as a writer and in the context of specific work that he would eventually submit for publication. The natural route for his self-sabotage was to compare himself with established and brilliant people that he admired and then proclaim that he "could not do it", "would never be good enough", etc. However, through a combination of our coaching work together, (which included a certain amount of cajoling), improved understanding and his commitment, he pulled through. As his confidence grew he was able to identify a compelling vision for his life ten years from now that allowed him to find the purpose that would achieve it. That was the key and although his resolve would still have the occasional wobble, the compass needle always settled quickly back at true North. Our e-mail correspondence was particularly volatile. He would rail at his own human failings, at the shame of his decline, at me for anything at all, be it challenging or supporting him. But he stuck to it. The hierarchy of his purpose was a constant reinforcement to any action he was required to take. He knew, however deeply, that inch by inch he could conquer the mountain, if instead of looking up or down he would just focus on where he was and do the next right thing in front of him. That was three years ago. Client confidentiality prevents me from naming the books that are now published and delighting children all over Europe. Suffice to say that they are and Toby can claim rightful ownership of authenticity and fulfilment as further evidence of his progress so far.

DISMANTLEMENT

However uncomfortable your life circumstances are, unless the whole edifice has already collapsed, knocking it down and re-building it brings its own emotional costs. Unsuitable it may be for your present needs, but familiar – definitely. The fear that paralyses most people in the process of mid life transition is either the anxiety that things might remain the same forever or that everything might change for good. Your commitment to a sustainable future can in part be measured by the extent to which you can emotionally commit to fundamental change, whatever that may involve. There is no pattern or template to observe here other than to implement whatever changes appear necessary to satisfy your evolving needs. Your intuitive response to these and the "creative environment" that you are seeking to build will be one of your guides as to how radical the re-build will have to be and what form it will eventually take. Listen to yourself. The voice of discontent may have been nagging at you for a while to tear down the walls, but what do you want to build in its place? If you have been unhappy, dissatisfied and unfulfilled in your work, what do you need to do to change that? The tools to help you answer the 7 Defining Questions of what you really, really want are here to help you in defining the supportive environment that you need to create for yourself. But be very aware. The actions that you take have to be informed by your intrinsic need for growth and generic creativity. Before you resign from your job, spend time establishing whether you are simply running away from something deeper. Doubtless, there will be something here to address and the tools here will assist you in that, but you will need to spend time here deciding and designing what form your new creative environment should take. Use your journal to expand on this. Let your mind roam free. Let thoughts and wishes become more concrete desires. Always though make the priority focus on how you want to BE. The details of how to DO this will come later.

PART 3

The New Beginning

People begin to become successful the minute they decide to be. - Harvey Mackay

Nothing has such a strong effect on children as the unlived life of a parent – Jung.

When you are inspired by some great purpose, some extraordinary project, all your thoughts break their bonds: your mind transcends limitations, your consciousness expands in every direction and you find yourself in a new, great, and wonderful world. Dormant forces, faculties and talents become alive and you discover yourself to be a greater person than you ever dreamed yourself to be. - Patanjali, Indian philosopher

If you want to build a ship, don't drum up the men to gather the wood, divide the work, and give orders. Instead, teach them to yearn for the vast and endless sea..
- Antoine de Saint Exupery

People over 65 were asked, 'If you could live your life over, what would you do differently?' They said three things: 'I'd take time to stop and ask the big questions. I'd be more courageous and take more risks in work and love. I'd try to live with purpose--to make a difference.' - Richard Leider, founding partner of the Inventure Group

The relevant question in looking at a job is not What will I do? But Who will I become?
                                                                                - Po Bronson

We shall not cease from exploring. And the end of all our exploring will be to arrive where we started and know the place for the first time. - T.S.Eliot

Listen to the inward voice and bravely obey that. Do the things at which you are great, not what you were never made for. - Ralph Waldo Emerson

THE JOURNEY TOWARDS RENEWAL

Re-entry into the world (and the entry into your new world) is unlikely to be accompanied by the gasping for air that accompanies submergence for an uncomfortably long time. Nor is it likely to be the deep, grateful lungfuls of a fresh air previously denied; the carbon monoxide of the city replaced by the ozone of the sea. Your breath of life will undergo a more subtle change than that, although no less profound. The dawning realisation that the air you breathe is becoming cleaner though could bring an awareness of other subtle changes: familiar things done differently, a new lightness to your manner, an attitude of gratitude for smaller things, or a sharpened perception to events and behaviours around you. You may find yourself more detached, forgiving, less judgmental. Your return is not to a place that has changed, but to somewhere very much the same. It is <u>you</u> who is different.

In a sense the Neutral Zone and the New Beginning have no barrier between them. It is more of an invisible boundary that separates the two, one that it is necessary to shuttle back and forth across to maintain constant reference to the grid co-ordinates. How am I compared to yesterday, last week, last month, last year? As with all other attributes of the mid life transition, it steadfastly denies us the satisfaction of a convenient checkpoint. There is no one day when you leave the Neutral Zone, only to find yourself satisfyingly installed at the point of a new beginning. Frustratingly, just as with all other aspects of your journey, there is also no predictable time frame to your crossing the border. Certainly, the journey is hastened by commitment and surrender; struggle will only keep you stuck. But never lose sight of the fact that this is a process of becoming with no obvious, finite end. Like the arrival of Spring, it is only a gradual realisation that green shoots and leaves are newly evident and birdsong louder that lets you know it has arrived. Only once you are truly through, can you look back and see where you have come from. And even then the process of your evolution continues. Just as a caterpillar undergoing its metamorphosis into a butterfly still has a life ahead of it once the process is complete, so your new way of being will be a continuation of the journey. Life will be less harsh. You will smell the flowers more. But it is not over. In fact, your journey to this place is the necessary preparation for you to really find out who you are now and fulfil the maximum potential of this new person. What an empowering, liberating prospect!

CREATIVITY

I have referred throughout to the concept of re-discovering your generic Creativity. The importance of pursuing this and ensuring its constant resonance in your new awareness cannot be emphasised enough. It is your one constant reference and the single quality that will ensure your long-term fulfillment.

A dictionary definition of "Creativity" gives us only this: "....relating to or involving the use of imagination or original ideas......." The natural extension of this for our purposes is more abstract. "Creativity" has a different subjective nuance for anyone seeking the fullest celebration and expression of their individuality. It allows us to deploy the use of our imagination and ingenuity in the tackling of not just tasks, but life itself. If our lives are lived with invention, imagination, vision, resourceful use of our natural talents and ingenuity, then normal everyday stresses instead become challenges to be attacked with enthusiasm. We are no longer engaged in a war of attrition with the day. Instead we are harmoniously in flow with it. We will come to Flow activities a little later. However, what I want to define here as an absolute is that "Creativity" as a generic term can inform all our lives *whoever we are and whatever we do*, once we align more with our true nature and recognise who we really are. It permeates and informs your very essence at every level. If your life can become an exploration of your own personal uniqueness and purpose, then your life will be lived as a delight.

The question you are asking yourself is: "Who are you now?" Your answer is likely to differ radically from your answer of twenty years ago. Experience has brought you perspective and wisdom, the World has altered and so has your place in it. Your needs have changed. This may mean that you need to change entirely what you do for a living in order to find that avenue of self-expression that you crave, or it could simply involve the subtlest but most powerful of changes to the way that you live your life already. Remember: first and foremost, it is about BEING. We all have a choice about the way that we approach our lives. To say otherwise is disempowering to you. Also it is not true. We all have a choice. How you exercise that choice will determine completely your place in the World and how you will be remembered. This process is about reclaiming the power that you have over your life and the way that you express your uniqueness. Sometimes it is just a flip of perception that enables an individual to see themselves and what they are entirely differently. A builder can see himself either as an unchallenged tradesman, or as the provider of exciting and interesting spaces for people to live in. He can choose to build unstimulating formatted shoe box houses, or he can explore the limitless range of architectural possibility. I have always envied builders. Everything they create is like a personal signature. I remember a builder that I employed once. He embodied all the qualities of creative satisfaction that I am describing. We were talking one day when he pointed out one of his masons engaged in the restoration of an old stone wall and said: "When he picks up a stone he knows where in the wall it belongs." The same builder had a foreman who would leave money secreted in every house he built, where it would eventually be found by the new occupants. Both of these men could have easily seen what they did simply as a full day's work for a full day's pay in the building trade. Yet they chose instead to live it. Each in his individual way found a way of expressing himself in and through his work. It was a delight to watch.

Answer these two questions:

- What does the word "Creative" mean for you?

- What is the biggest step you could take today towards living a more creative life?

A friend of mine once remarked to me that we are all defined more by what we turn away than by what we accept. He is right because therein lies the same empowerment of choice. If you decide not to go with the security of what is offered, but rather to take only those avenues that are congruent with your Values and creative self-expression, then your decision will have been to choose Being instead of Doing. And if you choose Being then Doing is in the details. Trust this.

SELF AWARENESS

To reinforce the foundations of such a utopian life requires that your self-awareness be optimised. Only through knowing and understanding yourself better can you go forward effectively without losing future momentum. So exactly what sort of person are you? There are many and varied tools to assist you in this and the findings can be enlightening. Your focus is on finding out WHO you are now. Ask yourself that question:

- Who am I now?

- What would have to change either subtly or radically about my life and the way that I live it for me to feel more in touch with the person that I am?

You may be the person you have always been – just more aware of not being in integrity with your own authentic self-expression. Or you may have altered profoundly over the last twenty years and realise that the way you live your life now has to make the same re-adjustments. So just WHO are you now....?

If that is a challenging question to which you find you have no immediately definitive response, do not be alarmed. During this threshold period, we can find ourselves yearning for a return to more familiar and secure territory conflicting with the pull of exciting new directions. Our personae can be equally torn. We find ourselves positioned somewhere between who we believe ourselves to have been, who we currently believe ourselves to be and who we have the potential to become. With our boundaries no longer secure, we are often vulnerable, tempted to cling to aspects of ourselves that are no longer appropriate. Yet just as tempting to us can be exploration of the unknown; a desire to explore the breadth of our as yet undiscovered, latent potential.

WHO AM I NOW?

It will help you to construct an objective view of the sort of person you are today and what has brought you to this point. What are the events that occurred along the way both, positive and negative that you remember? A good starting point is to fill out a timeline of your life through its different stages and note the events that you recall as having some formative significance for you. Do not search for any hidden meanings at this stage and do not try to prioritise the importance of events. Moving to your favourite house aged eleven and the happy times you remember there, is just as important as the relationship that you had with a favourite uncle for three years of your childhood. Likewise, the death of a sibling or parent is likely to have had a profound effect on you, but do not leave out how hurtful it was not being allowed to attend the school summer adventure camp. Both events affected you.

Using the timelines provided, chart your course to this point. You will see that for ease of use and reference, the stages of your life have been divided into five separate phases that range through early childhood to mid life. Complete all five including any events and memories that are of significance. You will find that memories of some things may trigger thoughts of other events. Let this be a releasing exercise for you. Enjoy the pleasure of re-entering the past and see what you learn. Below is a sample timeline to illustrate the way that you can approach this exercise. Take the time to remember back and see what thoughts and memories occur to you. Small memories may lead to bigger ones. The most important thing is to ignore your perception of how big or worthwhile recording an event was. Instead concentrate on the effect, positive or negative that it had on you. Do not leave anything out. Whatever the memory, if the event had an impact on you, record it. You may be surprised at how much you can remember once you have started.

EXAMPLE

YOUNG ADULT LIFE

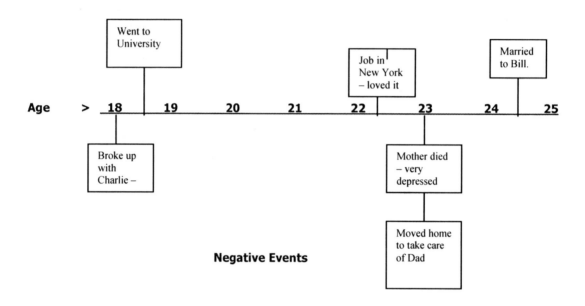

Now that you have a linear structure that begins to show your life's evolution to this point and some of the events that may have shaped it, look back carefully and add in more detail as it comes to mind. What thoughts occur to you? Is it glaringly obvious how and why you came to this point and the singular event(s) that precipitated your state, or do you see more of a teasing, subtle pattern at how you arrived? Or is it all still a mystery? Whatever your present summation, remember from earlier in this book that detail and events aside, you are taking responsibility from now on. This is a keystone to the solidity of your future success. You are no longer part of a blame culture that puts the responsibility for your happiness past, present or future outside of yourself. To do so is disempowering. It gives away the power over the gift of your personal happiness to someone or something else. YOU are in charge from now on. However tempting it is to say "But if....." ignore it. For whatever apparently cosmic reasons or sheer bad luck you find yourself where you are today, take back your power. Resolve that you take responsibility for yourself and your happiness from now on. You are in the driving seat. No single other thing, event or person is in charge of how happy and fulfilled you can be – YOU are.

CHILDHOOD

Positive events

Age >0 1 2 3 4 5 6 7 8 9 10 11

Negative events

CHILDHOOD/ADOLESCENCE

Positive events

Age > 11 12 13 14 15 16 17 18

Negative events

YOUNG ADULT LIFE

Positive events

Age > 18   19   20   21   22   23   24   25

Negative events

ADULT LIFE

Positive events

Age > 25   26   27   28   29   30   31   32   33   34

Negative events

112

MID LIFE

Positive events

Negative events

Age > **35**   **36**   **37**   **38**   **39**   **40**   **41**   **42**

Positive events

Negative events

Age   **>43**   **44**   **45**   **46**   **47**   **48**   **49**   **50**

113

Write down a frank assessment of the person you are today with the attributes and strengths that you possess. Define your qualities and also your (perceived) shortcomings, although be kind. This is a constructive exercise. Do not "should" on yourself though by looking for qualities or attributes that you feel you "should" have. It is very important that you avoid this as it will inevitably make you feel less than you are and is not constructive. Just give an accurate picture. This is not a quest for unrealisable perfection. It is a real attempt at re-defining you for the future and the path you wish to pursue. Acknowledge your strengths and notice those areas where you could benefit from work or practice to improve. Leave nothing out.

The person I am today is--

What is the picture that you are now confronted with? How do you feel about the person in front of you now? Can you see that despite the peaks and troughs that may be evident from your life journey, how much experience you have now that qualifies you to move beyond where you find yourself? You are where you need to be. And just as importantly, you are able to move towards where you want to go. If you add the experience and attributes that you demonstrate to the emerging clarity of your new persona and the destinations that are possible, you are looking at an individual with everything they need to succeed.

Earlier you answered questions relating to the roles that you played in your life. Having identified those I invited you to ask yourself "Why?" 5 times to those questions. Review your answers now thoughtfully and then answer the questions here that follow. As with all of these questionnaires, allow yourself to do this in an atmosphere or environment that encourages clear thought without distraction. Try hard to answer all the questions, although if you find that you do not have an answer, leave it and move on. This is an ongoing process and you can return to it at a later point. However, do not seek either definitive answers where there are none, or some acceptable compromise that ducks the issue. This work is for you alone and very importantly it does not have to conform to a newly defined role that has other people in mind when defining it. Do not project into the future about how fundamental changes might affect others, or have any concerns about how others might react to your answers. You will have an opportunity to rationalise this later. For now though, answer the questions honestly without forethought. Follow your feelings.

- If I could change my role today, what would I become?

- If I had the choice, what would I keep and what would I discard in my life?

- What new aspects of my persona do I want to fully embrace?

- How would I describe my new persona?

- Who am I (or becoming) now?

Further assistance in defining who you are now can also be found through personality profiling, psychometric testing and using some form of typology as a guide. Meyers-Briggs (MBTI), Enneagrams and other personality typing aids can be very useful. There is no doubt for me that individuals can derive benefit from doing this as well and I would not discourage the insights that these can provide. In the hands of an expert they can be illuminating and sometimes I use them myself with clients where it feels appropriate. However, the journey towards authenticity starts and ends with you and responsibility for that cannot be devolved to a third party. It is your instinct and developing intuition that will lead you to the gate of renewal. By all means seek additional insights into your personality type and the benefits that they can confer. But do this work first. Trust your own inner wisdom.

WRITE YOUR OWN OBITUARY

However, alarming the prospect of doing this might be to you, give it due attention. If you tackle this exercise it can be both revealing and cathartic. Write in the third person, as though a good friend who knew you well and very fondly, but with a retained objectivity, had taken on the task of committing your life to history. What unlived potential, expectations, beliefs, and talents had been wasted as a result of your early demise? At the point where in a several million to one freak accident the tree struck by lightning fell on your rental car, where were you...? Were you navigating the Neutral Zone but with a feeling that there was at least light at the end of the tunnel? Were you paralysed with an unquantifiable terror, petrified that nothing would change or worse that everything would? Had you attained a premise of some new understanding, or did nothing make any more sense than ten years ago? Perhaps you were poised in realisation. Or were you retreating into the emptiness that so characterises this phase of transition? Be generous in your praise of everything thus far achieved and tolerant of things still outstanding. Do not discount the love of family and friends and the qualities that they adored in you. Acknowledge yourself. Take some delight in being able to hear what would have been said about you and being there to hear it! In describing what your unfulfilled potential had been, you are outlining your hope for the future once you have navigated this territory. There will be a future.

Whatever your state, be accepting of it. As you know now, there is no right or wrong way to do this, so whatever the experience initiates in you, embrace it wholly and be prepared to surrender to its journey. Like Beowulf earlier, the trust to disarm yourself and rely on your own inherent strengths to carry you through is the greatest test.

CREATE YOUR OWN RITE OF PASSAGE

For those individuals engaged in transition, there is a need for understanding as well as many and varied options for formulating a coping strategy. The transition process at mid life requires surrender. If society has not equipped you with an intuitive understanding of the benefits that accrue from returning to primal chaos, this can be very challenging. This instinctive grasp in other cultures has often come from ritual and the symbolism of rite of passage. It may be inadvisable to try and bolt on some similar ceremony from another culture as we have already discussed, but it does not prevent individuals engaging with an aspect of their own creativity in seeking to access more of it. If it feels helpful, create your own ceremony or ritual. Involve others if that feels appropriate or carry it out on your own. You may find yourself mining a rich seam of "otherness" that temporarily transcends your present sense of cultural identity. Whatever you feel moved to create – do it. The power that accompanies such self-identification can be immense. Feel free to borrow from whatever shamanic or American Indian traditions as feel right for you. Or newly invent your own. Burn an effigy of your former life, stroke yourself with eagle feathers, undergo a re-birth walking through fire, make incantations and beat drums in the sweat lodge, dig your own grave and endure the overwhelm of laying down in it overnight. Whatever action - if anything – feels appropriate to you and embeds you in the experience, embrace it. The altered state of consciousness that you attain through staying up for 24 hours may be the only time in your life that you have abandoned yourself to YOU in this way. Whatever you do though and in whatever grand, ethnic style – please do it safely. The whole point of this is to usher in a new era; to mark a crossing over. Being injured or worse in the process rather negates the point of doing it.

WHAT DO YOU WANT?

Go back to the 7 Defining Questions (Page 49) that you began to answer earlier. How do your responses look to you now? Do you feel you still want the same things? Is there an increased clarity now to your answers? Does the possibility of having the things you want excite you? If you have not done so already, complete this section. Be as comprehensive in your answers as possible. You have a lifetime opportunity to define EXACTLY what it is that you want for your life from now on. You have the experience and acquired wisdom now to really take yourself forward - IF you can define clearly what it is that you want for your life. If you have not done so already, give this the deepest of thought. Answer the questions fully and see what comes up. Do not edit or censor your responses in any way. Amaze yourself with the possibilities of where this might take you.

Inevitably, your answers to the 7 Defining Questions will mean that some aspects of your life will have to fundamentally change. This is a challenging demand. What are the things though that you want to change for good? Which things will never feature again in your life because your horizon now looks so different? Define absolutely for yourself what you are going to change, (or have to change), forever. Before you reach the Foundation Tools section and begin to conduct a general de-cluttering and streamlining of your life to give it increased manageability, look closely at the general picture. Understand that to go forward in the way that you would like to, some things will have to change - permanently. What elements of your life do you want to (and are prepared to), dispense with forever?

Do not underestimate the challenge of such a simple question. Pursuit of your authenticity and putting happiness and fulfilment at the top of your list will involve some radical changes. You have to be prepared to make them and at some point it will involve courage on your part. Be realistic and rational. Nothing is impossible to the committed individual. Problems become challenges once you have a vision. Take stock of how some of these decisions might affect family, lifestyle, geographical location of where you are living and plan for them. Seek practical and pragmatic solutions where appropriate and consider radical options where these may be necessary. Open yourself up to possibilities of change and growth. Expand your horizon to include all possibilities. Make a list of all your options for consideration.

MIND MAP

This is a useful exercise created by Tony Buzan that allows for an expansion of your thought processes without the linear constraints of compiling a list. It is a creative way of both planning and problem solving. Using this example, follow your thought processes and explore the different influences on your life and career to see where they lead. As well as providing an opportunity to easily pursue a train of thought and see where it goes, it also allows you to pinpoint the specific areas of satisfaction and dissatisfaction that have influence in your life. You can use the table that follows over the page to give this further clarity. The main facility of this is that you can allow simple connections to be made between seemingly unconnected thoughts and see where they lead. Very often an apparently random thought can have far more relevance to a situation and its understanding or solution than you would expect and certainly would not appear as part of a linear exploration. Let your mind roam freely and see what surfaces...

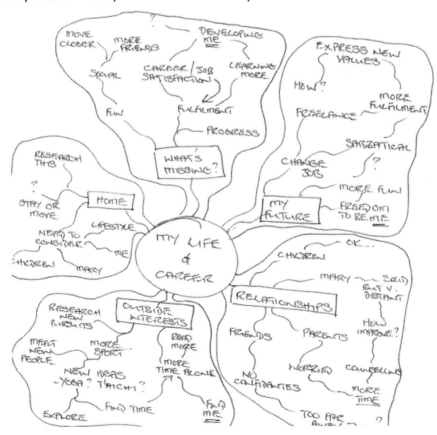

SUMMARY OF SATISFIERS AND DISSATISFIERS

It may be of use to you to formalise the elements of satisfaction and dissatisfaction in your life. The smaller details of things you are tolerating will be dealt with later on. However, it will be important to you to clarify the acceptable facts of your life in black and white. Even if you feel that are clear about these already, complete the tables so that no facts or elements are pushed to one side. If you are not clear, using these tables will help you achieve more clarity.

Major Satisfiers

JOB People	Activities
1.	1.
2.	2.
3.	3.
4.	4.
CAREER People	Activities
1.	1.
2.	2.
3.	3.
4.	4.
LIFE People	Activities
1.	1.
2.	2.
3.	3.
4.	4.

Major Dissatisfiers

JOB People	Activities
1.	1.
2.	2.
3.	3.
4.	4.
CAREER People	Activities
1.	1.
2.	2.
3.	3.
4.	4.
LIFE People	Activities
1.	1.
2.	2.
3.	3.
4.	4.

Although this is a rather clinical analysis, for those of you in doubt, it provides incontrovertible evidence of where you may need to start in your pursuit of an environment that provides you with more satisfaction and conversely where you could seek to make changes.

PROJECT INTO YOUR FUTURE IDEAL LIFE

In a separate exercise describe the TYPE of life that you see yourself involved in. As we have discussed before, this is an opportunity for you to give your imagination full rein. There are no wrong answers to how this looks or the detail it contains. Even if you do not know yet specifically what your future occupation will be, or you know that any changes you make will not involve an employment shift, describe the feeling, the elemental attractions, the texture of it. But be specific. Just saying Rich, Fat and Happy is not enough. What kind of "Rich", how "Fat", "Happy" doing what? And why...? Your description needs to be sensory rich. Make it live for yourself. See yourself in this new world and describe it to yourself fully. If the question of money comes up (and for a lot of people it does), examine the question of what wealth means to you. Most people if asked will say that they want more money. But how much more? What specifically do you want to achieve with more wealth? Before you decide that the life you want is that of a billionaire, examine why. If "more money" simply means "financial independence" then examine your issues around security. If it means enough to have holidays, a second home, to eat in a restaurant whenever you choose and play golf twice a week, you may not need to become a multi-millionaire to achieve that. I do not wish to limit your aspirations and there is nothing wrong with any of us having more money when we use it well. However, it is important to be clear about what you want and why you want it. The difference between a billion dollars and a growing income that can generate in excess of a million could potentially involve a lot of needless time or effort. If it is only financial independence that you seek to remove the spectre of lack, then focus on EXACTLY how much you will realistically need and factor this into your aspirations. Just doing this brings it immediately closer and adds more substance. On the other hand, if it is a billion dollars that you need or aspire to and you can justify this with the vision of your future life purpose, then plan and strategise with the achievement of this in mind.

The main thrust of this exercise though is to explore your right livelihood in pursuit of you leading an authentic life. This is a powerful exercise and can show you a glimpse of the future. Focus on the kind of life that you wish to pursue. If you are a lawyer and you see yourself as a boat builder, see yourself IN that life. Imagine the satisfactions of crafting something so beautiful and the labour of love that it could involve. What decisions are involved? Would you have to live by the coast? Where could you see yourself living? What kind of boats are you building and for whom? If you do not yet have the requisite skills, see yourself acquiring them. Begin to see the strategy that you will have to implement to do this and to take yourself forward.

My ideal life---

SET YOUR GOALS

There are thousands of books on Goal Setting. My own influences have been wide ranging in this area – Jim Rohn, Dr. Michael Anthony, Napoleon Hill, are just part of a very long list. They endorse my view completely that the practice of Goal Setting is key to the achievement of your Life Purpose. And this as part of your recovery in the latter stages of mid life transition will be crucial to your sustained progress.

Earlier you defined your Life Purpose and looked at Time Management processes that would help you achieve it. The next step then is to identify what are the incremental goals that have to be achieved for you to fulfil your lofty ambition to the lasting benefit of yourself and those others that may be affected. The step process below can be used for the achievement of all goals that you set, whether they are part of your Life Purpose or not. However, it is likely by now that any goals you have identified will have a natural place in your hierarchy of purpose, because at some level they will be interwoven into the bigger picture. When you have perfect clarity on this you are ready for an achievement strategy. You are ready to identify the building blocks to your success and to achieve those incremental goals that will take you across the threshold. In Coaching terms, this means that we move from Vision to Mission. Take a look at the process here and once you have absorbed it, you can move into action.

- STEP 1. Identify the goals and objectives that will be necessary to take you forward and ultimately help you achieve the outcomes you desire. Write them down in detail.
- STEP 2. Prioritise these in the necessary order and give them a time frame for their achievement. Use a year planner or Gantt chart to give this a linear focus.
- STEP 3. Identify the skills or qualities you will need to successfully accomplish each incremental goal. Be detailed about these.
- STEP 4. Make detailed plans to acquire any specific skills or to practise existing ones to a sufficiently high standard.
- STEP 5. Incorporate the time lines for all of the above into a colourful, detailed map of where you are heading and put it where you will always see it. Add to this at will.

Any goals that you set should be SMART goals, that is:

Sustainable – Manageable – Achievable – Realistic – Time-framed.

- STEP 1. Identify the goals and objectives that will be necessary to take you forward and ultimately help you achieve the outcomes you desire. Make this a ten-year plan. Enter them in detail in the table below so that they have a real resonance for you. Then group the answers as indicated.

ONE YEAR GOALS	THREE YEAR GOALS
1.	1.
2.	2.
3.	3.
4.	4.
5.	5.
6.	6.
7.	7.
8.	8.
9.	9.
10.	10.
FIVE YEAR GOALS	TEN YEAR GOALS
1.	1.
2.	2.
3.	3.
4.	4.
5.	5.
6.	6.
7.	7.
8.	8.
9.	9.
10.	10.

When setting out your goals, be sure that these are objectives that you want to work towards achieving NOW, not historical objectives that remain unachieved and which are attached to some previous agenda. For example, if you are seeking a specific promotion at work, be sure of why you want it and remember that we started this book discussing the necessity of Being before Doing. Do not look outside of yourself for external stimuli to bring you gratification. The purpose of these goals is to satisfy and affirm you. They will not be charged with the responsibility of making you happy.

How does that list look to you now? Does it excite you? Do you feel energised to take action in pursuit of achieving these goals? GOOD.

- STEP 2. Choose the three most important goals from each category and enter them here. You have already given a time frame for the achievement of this, so your next objective is to develop a strategy. Alongside each write down the first three steps that you will have to take to move this goal forward.

ONE YEAR GOALS	ACHIEVEMENT STRATEGY
1.	1.
	2.
	3.
2.	1.
	2.
	3.
3.	1.
	2.
	3.

THREE YEAR GOALS	ACHIEVEMENT STRATEGY
1.	1.
	2.
	3.
2.	1.
	2.
	3.
3.	1.
	2.
	3.

FIVE YEAR GOALS	ACHIEVEMENT STRATEGY
1.	1.
	2.
	3.
2.	1.
	2.
	3.
3.	1.
	2.
	3.

TEN YEAR GOALS	ACHIEVEMENT STRATEGY
1.	1.
	2.
	3.
2.	1.
	2.
	3.
3.	1.
	2.
	3.

- STEP 3. Identify the skills or qualities you will need to successfully accomplish each incremental goal. Be detailed about these and how you are going to accomplish these tasks. If for example you had to learn a language, would that require complete fluency or would conversational level suffice. Is there a requirement for jargon or specialised vocabulary? Explore this step in as much detail as necessary.

ONE YEAR GOALS   WHAT I NEED TO LEARN OR DO BETTER

-----------------------------   --
-----------------------------   --
-----------------------------   --

THREE YEAR GOALS   WHAT I NEED TO LEARN OR DO BETTER

-----------------------------   --
-----------------------------   --
-----------------------------   --

FIVE YEAR GOALS	WHAT I NEED TO LEARN OR DO BETTER
--------------------------	---
--------------------------	---
--------------------------	---

TEN YEAR GOALS	WHAT I NEED TO LEARN OR DO BETTER
--------------------------	---
--------------------------	---
--------------------------	---

- STEP 4. Make detailed plans to acquire any specific skills or to practise existing ones to a sufficiently high standard. Might it be possible to learn your new language at the same time as acquiring other skills? Plan your campaign in rigorous and infinite detail. Failing to prepare is preparing to fail. It would be a tragedy if having identified the life of your dreams that your future outcomes were let down by bad planning. Spend time and energy on this. The more effort and ingenuity that you put into this now, the greater success you will reap. Do this in conjunction with the Future Timeline exercise that follows. You can incorporate the results into Step 5.

- STEP 5. Incorporate the time lines for all of the above into a colourful, detailed map of where you are heading and put it where you will see it constantly. Add to this all the time. This map will never be perfect and it is not designed to be. This is the road map to your destination. Regard it always as work in progress that can be adjusted and amended as necessary. Write resonant affirmations on it that will reinforce both you and the meaningfulness of your purpose. Make this your favourite picture to look at. Put anything at all on it that might strengthen the image. This picture typifies your resolve and declares your direction unequivocally. However, things change and often for the better. So prepare from the start to be flexible, although without losing your focus. If you have a five or ten-year plan, it is unlikely that everything will work out *exactly* as you planned. But if you accept your newly found capacity to see obstacles as challenges that you CAN transcend, your purpose will not weaken.

Remember: Vision to Mission to Goal. You have established a bigger picture for where you want to be and how you see your life a good distance from now. Those of you who have gained clarity through your endurance of these testing times will be able to see yourselves ten years from now or more. Others of you will be on the way to achieving this. Wherever you are on the journey, those images of your future will become sensory-rich in every way. You are beginning to run *towards* the future rather than *away* from your present and as you do so will be able to see, feel, smell the world as you approach it. And that world begins today as you set the incremental goals for taking yourself forward and creating it. Be rigorous in establishing the primacy of the achievement these. The core activity of making constant progress towards achieving a life of fulfilment is paramount.

MOLLY

Molly is an example of a brilliant self-motivating individual who has achieved an enormous amount in later life, yet is prevented from really fulfilling her potential because she is mesmerised by her own activity. If anyone puts Doing before Being - it is Molly.

Now in her early fifties she has devoted herself in later life to a new career as a lawyer. Having transcended the trauma of a marriage breakdown, she picked herself up and moved on. In a very short time she has not only qualified as a solicitor, but also served her articles and set up a law practice on her own that employs eight other solicitors and enough staff to service them – a formidable achievement. However, this is not enough for Molly. She is grooming her children to take over the practice, at which point she has dreams of historic property development, opening a health spa, learning to drive a coach and pair and travelling the World. (At the moment she never takes a holiday).

When we started working together, Molly's main obstruction to moving away from the all-consuming activity of overseeing the running of her practice – was Molly. She could not get out of her own way, which was intriguing because she had accomplished so much in a short time. She had hit a potentially arresting plateau. Finding it nearly impossible to delegate high level decision-making, she would watch over her younger office staff like a broody hen and spend every day so tied up with the responsibilities of her job (and everyone else's), that she could never make time for herself. The practice was growing exponentially, which was a goal in itself, but with its successful expansion came added workload. The consequence of this was that Molly could not find a moment even to think and plan what she wanted to do next.

The basis that we evolved for working together was predicated on the simple fact that if she did not put herself and her self-care first then, she could not hope to be her best for all the people who needed her. So we evolved a self-care regime including exercise that would achieve this. In a very short time indeed the increased vitality that Molly experienced and the very obvious primacy that was being given to meeting her needs, sent out a strong message: "I come first and everything is better as a result". A big part of this was working hard on her time management to ensure that she could prioritise her tasking and ensure that enough time was being allocated to her core activity of evolving a strategy for the future. Molly had come up with a real vision for where she saw herself in ten years and in order to realise the full potential of this, she had to allocate time for working towards and achieving the goals that would bring it closer. This meant that core activity time, (which included working with me), had to be ring-fenced so that nothing would divert her from her purpose. We worked with the same highly effective but simple colour coding time management system that gave a clear demarcation to the different strands of Molly's day. Very simply, any time allocated to core activity was given priority and treated as an unbreakable appointment. After all, she would not miss a client meeting, so why would she miss an appointment with someone as important as herself? After all, she was the only one who could propel her towards a more rewarding future.

The net gains of this new discipline were immediate. With everything oriented around a big picture of the future, the day to day demands on her time had to be resolved very effectively. Boundaries around her availability were introduced. People were given very specific time slots for meetings, appointments had to be made instead of the previous open door policy that had prevailed and a raft of delegation measures was introduced to liberate the time necessary for her to concentrate on specific issues. This had the additional benefit of incentivising her practice and office managers who thrived with the new autonomy and responsibility. With a clear vision for where she wanted to go and the discipline to adhere to the new system, Molly was set for realistic and manageable progress towards her goals.

As with the example of Molly above, I want to stress that it really is possible to lead a balanced life that allows time and space for you to work hard on your goals as well as have time for those close to you that require your love and attention. It simply takes the effort. Not struggle, just effort and desire – and rigorous discipline.

FUTURE TIMELINE

The exercise that you completed earlier using timelines that brought you to the present day can now be followed to a logical conclusion. Your efforts thus far in establishing what you want and why you want it have been enshrined in a powerful declaration of your personal purpose and you have set the goals that you want to achieve, backed up by a realistic strategy for achieving them. So the next step is to SEE your future going forward in the way that you predict.

Draw a timeline from today that shows the order of events that you predict in moving towards your future. It can be helpful to make this part of your Life Map. Your strategy will help you here. The incremental goals that you have set yourself to accomplish are all factored into a plan. Whatever realistic assessment you have made as part of Step 2 for the time you will take to achieve these, can now be used as a benchmark indicator. If you mark down the future progress that you expect to make and the time that you will take to do so, you will quickly see where the lapses in your efficacy might occur through taking too long to achieve a certain stage. If this seems likely then put in an additional stage. So for example, if your future livelihood requires you to become qualified in some way and this will take say a year, break down the year into individual parts that form part of achieving your qualification. This will help to keep your motivation high until you pass your examinations. Work with this in conjunction with your life map until you have a realistic timeline and also one that really inspires you. If you know today that in only two years you can expect to be living a life worth living and that with the successful achievement of your strategy, in five years you will have the life of your dreams, you might expect to feel elated. After all, how long were you engaged in a life that did <u>not</u> satisfy you?!

So as with the previous timelines that you have completed to give yourself a picture of what events have characterised your journey to this point, enter the details of your future. Put in all the relevant detail and inspire yourself to take action. Add this to your life map and allow it to endorse even further the action steps that you will take in going forward.

FOUNDATION TOOLS

Manageability is a key to your progress, to continued growth, sustained focus and unassailable self-esteem. All of these elements will be essential to the rock solid foundations of the structure you are building. So become manageable. Dealing with your TOLERATIONS, undertaking a DUST BUST of your life and making an objective assessment of the five key areas of your life – Time, Energy, Money, Love and Space (to be yourself), in this adaptation of THE WHEEL OF LIFE will allow you to do just that. Once you have tackled these fundamental tasks fully and are ready to commit to a constant maintenance of them, you are ready to start building.

So in constructive pursuit of Being, here are three tools to consolidate the foundations. Conduct a Dust Busting spring clean of your life, eradicate all Tolerations and check to make sure that the key areas of your life are in balance. Work with these tools consistently. Contract with yourself to make time every week, to review and to see where you might set a new goal to accomplish, or make an improvement to those areas of your life that support you. This discipline could be the difference between your future happiness being possible or probable. Would you put the Wheel of Life you have drawn on your car? Or would the ride be too bumpy to contemplate? Take action.

Conducting an audit of all areas of your life does in some ways allow a personal diagnostic assessment. It shows clearly the areas that need strengthening and allows you to conduct a clearance of those small things or issues that at some level might be draining your energy. If you can achieve some positive clearance, this will allow you to correspondingly strengthen your energy and resolve, reduce your stress, increase your focus on important issues and help you to attract better people and opportunities into your life. So shake things up – radically!

" Maintaining a complicated life is a great way to avoid changing it"

– Elaine St. James

Dust Bust Your Life

Conducting a radical spring clean of your life may not be an immediately apparent strategy for the pursuit of authentic self-expression and personal fulfillment. However, as with Tolerations, You will be surprised at the difference and empowerment that comes with tackling and resolving the smallest of things, as well as the increase in energy when you orient your lifestyle around greater personal self-efficacy. This might be achieved through something as simple as evolving a new filing system to support you better and allow immediate access to whatever you need, or it could come with having the full physical examination from your doctor that you have been putting off for so long. Take a holistic approach now to your life. Since you have decided to BE, this new You needs to be in the best condition with a fully operational and supportive infrastructure.

Without being too prescriptive, let us take a look at some of the areas where this might be achieved. If as a result of giving this attention other thoughts occur to you, tackle these right away too. You will know instinctively which additional areas might require attention. Be ruthless and rigorous. Leave no area of your life alone that you feel will not support your progress.

HEALTH

- I am aware of everything that I have to do to maintain a
  healthy lifestyle that supports me, including exercise.   ----   ----   ----
  *Regular exercise manages stress and releases endorphins
  into our blood stream, giving us a feeling of happiness and
  well-being. More energy, another benefit of exercise means
  we can achieve more and with that comes a self-esteem
  boosting sense of accomplishment.*

- All medical and dental checks are up to date, including eye
  tests and cholesterol/blood pressure counts.   ----   ----   ----
  *For some, a tendency to suffer anxiety and worry about
  anything, can create worries where none exist. Feeling
  assured and confident about our health helps us to focus
  concern in a more productive way.*

- My alcohol consumption is low and I avoid the use of
  harmful substances.   ----   ----   ----
  *Alcohol and drugs can cause us to feel depressed among
  other negative long-term effects. Be kind to yourself and
  reduce your intake. Using these as a medication for stress
  will have no positive impact on your long-term optimism.*

- I allocate plenty of time through the year for holidays and
  exercise real self-care regularly, (massage, walks, etc.)   ----   ----   ----
  *To maintain a healthy life, we need to control our stress
  levels. Taking time out from a busy life to rest and do the
  things that bring us pleasure, gives the mind and body a
  restorative break.*

- I have a loving and rewarding home life that I nurture and that in return brings me great joy.   ----   ----   ----

  Research shows that people who have loving, happy relationships fight disease better and live longer.

ENVIRONMENT

- My home and office filing systems perfectly support me and are completely up to date.   ----   ----   ----

  Clutter in the home or office can create mental distraction and overload, having implications on short and long term memory that distract the focus from peak performance.

- My car and all Home and Office appliances are in perfect working order.   ----   ----   ----

  The practical downside of equipment failure is a loss of productive time and focus. There is no good time for something to go wrong. The impact of this happening will cost you more than a good maintenance contract.

- My Home and Office environments are inspiring, creative spaces to live and work and are in a geographical location of my choice.   ----   ----   ----

  Choose home and work environments that inspire you. You can not be expansively creative or approach peak performance unless you are in surroundings to nurture this.

- There is an abundance of light and air in my living and working environment.   ----   ----   ----

  Light and clear space allow energy to flow freely. De-clutter your life. Create the right environment for positive change and optimal performance.

- I always have adequate time for everything I do. I am consistently early for appointments.   ----   ----   ----

  Running late causes us to feel stressed, releasing adrenaline and Cortisol into the blood stream. The "fight or flight" response results in unnecessary energy loss that leaves us feeling tired once we have calmed down. Releasing Cortisol, which protects the immune system, can mean that we do not have enough left over to fight off illness. That extra 10 minutes could cost you more than an apology!

FINANCES

- I save at least 10% of my income after deductions and have reserves equivalent to 6 months earnings in a readily accessible account.   ----   ----   ----

  Embark on a strategy to accomplish this. You are living through testing times. Financial reserves are important to fall back on where necessary and once you have formed the habit, the long term benefits will be worthwhile.

- My finances are manageable and I have a realistic plan for eradicating any outstanding debts.   ----   ----   ----

  Peak performance is about focused attention – knowing where to direct attention to achieve results is what makes us successful. Do not allow yourself to be distracted by financial irritations or pressures.

- I have comprehensive insurance for everything. I have no untoward anxiety over loss or damage.   ----   ----   ----

  Remove those elements of surprise that can trip you up when things feel they are going well.

- I know my worth and I have a strategy for achieving financial
  independence.   ----   ----   ----

  *As above. Your successful navigation through mid life is
  dependent on removing those external pressures that can
  divert your focus. Looking to the future involves being able
  to see what it looks like. Develop a strategy for financial
  independence and your focus on an authentic future will
  be even sharper.*

- There are no unresolved legal disputes or wrangles
  hanging over my life.   ----   ----   ----

  *Resolve anything that might impinge on your focused
  attention. Legal disputes can be draining and exhausting
  – hardly the nourishment that your creative soul needs!*

RELATIONSHIPS

- I have good relations with my family, friends and co -
  workers. My life is lived on my terms and not by the
  preferences of others.   ----   ----   ----

  *Expectations of others and our significant others can put
  us under pressure that has no benefit for us. Worrying
  about making others happy means that we do not get
  what WE want. Look after yourself for them and let them
  look after themselves for you.*

- I release myself from judgement of others. I can separate
  a person from their actions and look for the best in people. ----   ----   ----

  *Since we can never really know what others are thinking or
  what drives them, try to use empathy and endow them with
  positive characteristics. Try this. You will feel more positive
  and people will respond to you in that way too.*

- There are no draining relationships in my life. I spend time only with people who inspire or love me unconditionally.   ----   ----   ----

  As you discover more about the new and emerging YOU, your need to be affirmed and supported by those who have your best interests at heart is paramount. Let go of people who do not support you or have a vested interest only in keeping you as they need you to be.

- I quickly resolve misunderstandings and arguments. I tell the truth and take responsibility for what is heard or understood.   ----   ----   ----

  Research shows that we replay and re-visit negative incidents over and over in our minds in a way that we do not with positive ones. Disagreements can rent space in our heads, leaving less room for positive, forward progress.

- I communicate clearly my personal needs to others and ensure that these are met where necessary.   ----   ----   ----

  Leave no doubt in your mind about this. The route to success in any effective verbal or non-verbal communication lies in giving clear messages that minimise stressful and distracting arguments later over apportioning blame and misunderstandings.

Award yourself points for your answers: 2 points = Yes/Not applicable

                                                1 point = Sometimes

                                                0 points = No.

DATE: ---- ---- ----   DATE: ---- ---- ----   DATE: ---- ---- ----

SCORE =   SCORE =   SCORE =

Take the test now and then set a monthly date for re-taking it until you are at 75% or higher. Set a monthly target of at least 2 new statements to be completely true.

Whatever the speed of your progress - be kind to yourself.

Tolerations

Identify anything at all, (including your own behaviour), that you are tolerating rather than dealing with. Whether this is a small issue or one that has assumed disproportionate importance, put it on your list and resolve to eradicate it. It could be a leaking tap that needs attending to, a picture gathering dust that is waiting to be hung on the wall, or taking the time to file your tax return. Deal with it and tick it off your list. The change that accompanies such actions is phenomenal. The act of tolerating even the smallest of things rents space in your head that could be free for more important use. Actively dealing with your Tolerations energises you to attack the future and move away forcibly from the past.

I am Tolerating:

1. _____

2. _____

3. _____

4. _____

5. _____

6. _____

7. _____

8. _____

9. _____

10. _____

List your Tolerations above and implement a swift plan to blitz them. No matter how large or small the item – deal with it. From now on make an appointment with yourself to both list and deal with Tolerations on a weekly basis. Set aside the same time every week if you can, to make sure that everything is dealt with immediately. If this is not possible, plan ahead so that this time is allocated in your diary for the weeks to come to achieve this.

Wheel of Life

Take a look at the "Wheel of Life" diagram here. This tool is designed to show where areas of your life might be out of balance, the idea being that once you have scored yourself honestly on these, that you then connect those scores to form a wheel. It will be very evident to you straightaway whether the wheel you have now drawn is capable of giving you a smooth ride or not. The bigger and rounder the wheel, the smoother the ride, the smaller and more out of shape….. ! Use this tool as well under more specific headings if that feels more appropriate for you. For example, you could have the spokes represent Relationships, Career, Prosperity, Health, Future Plans, or any other area that seems pertinent. Whatever you choose to address, the important outcome you seek is balance.

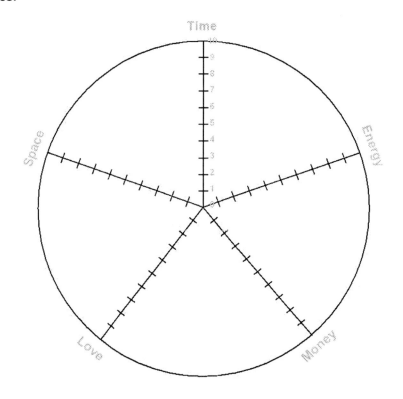

In Coaching these are useful tools to make sure that there is no barrier between a client and the goals they set. For you to pursue a life that is now based on the Values that you wish to express and a Purpose you believe in, nothing can be allowed to deflect you. Remember the Hierarchy of Purpose that we looked at a little earlier. Unless the purpose of an activity you are engaged in endorses the greater purposes of your life through your Values, or satisfies a Need, then however important it might seem at the time, it has a secondary priority to other pursuits. Be rigorous about maintaining this standard. So having scored your life on the Wheel of Life diagram, it is now important that you take the steps necessary to give yourself an improving score. Go back to the other tools in this section and make sure that you have itemised both the source of your dissatisfaction and the action steps necessary to change this.

SELF CARE

The area of constant self-care is one of the most challenging to implement and is usually one of the easiest to let slide down your list of priorities. Yet it is one of the most fundamental to your long-term success. There are a number of obstacles to committing to your self-care:

- You feel that you may appear selfish
- Apparent lack of time
- Misunderstanding its importance

Let us deal with these in order.

In order for you to be the best you can be for other people, you have to be the best You. If you are not at your best, you become a drain on the energy of others and however well-intentioned you are, you will deplete those that need your support. Jim Rohn is fond of saying: "I'll look after myself for you, if you look after yourself for me". That is the most complete way of summing up this philosophy that I can think of. When you travel on an aeroplane and the cabin staff advise you of the safety procedures, one of the things they point out is that if the oxygen supply should fail, then masks will drop down for your use. They then emphasise that parents should fit their OWN masks before attending to their children. The reasons are obvious and they are the same as those that we need to apply to our everyday self-care. If we lose consciousness the child will have no one looking after it. If we are fully taken care of, we can take proper care of them both immediately and in the long-term. So in considering what you need to optimise your faculties, emotional welfare and physical well-being, make the implementation of these a priority before anything else.

If there is not enough time for your self-care, either make a rigorous assessment of your time management, (we touched on this earlier) or delegate tasks to others that are taking up too much of your time. Whether at work or at home, the focus is on you being the best that you can be. Do not be a martyr to your staff or your family and do not avoid delegating based on the perception that no one can carry out a task better than you. Teach others to do it as well as you – and use the extra time for your self-care.

The importance of self-care is one that will make more sense to you with increased practice. At some level, to practise self-care sends a message to you and others that you are important; that your self worth deserves to be high. It demonstrates unequivocally that you are of value and your actions in perpetuating your value substantiate this. Other people receive the same message, both consciously and sub-consciously. In committing to your self as a priority you send out a strong signal of the strength of your self-esteem. Beware of others trying to undermine this. It is a natural instinct that people with lower self worth than you may put effort into pulling you back to where they are so that they feel more comfortable. Be ready to help others at all times – as long as YOUR Needs are fully met; and one of those needs is for your self-care to be optimal.

Make a list of 10 daily habits that automatically make you and the day feel better. Usually, these are the first things that we forget to do for ourselves when we are in a hurry. This could be something as simple as smelling the roses in your garden as you leave for work or observing your daily yoga and meditation routine. Perhaps you enjoy taking 10 minutes for a cup of coffee after taking the children to school, or making time to get away from your desk at lunch time. Perhaps it is a long hot bath at the end of the day in essential oils. Whatever your favourite things are, make a list of 10 that really make a difference to you and how the day feels when you include them. Now make a list of 52 things that are a treat and that you would like to do once a week, say a trip to a theatre or cinema, booking a massage, buying flowers for yourself. (If you cannot come up with 52 then try 26 – you can repeat them all). List them. Now list 12 things that you would like to do on a monthly basis such as a weekend away with your loved one, or a solitary retreat to a health spa. Finally make a list of 4 things that are an even bigger treat such as exotic holidays that you could spoil yourself with once every three months. If you want to complete the sequence in style, decide on one thing that you could do for yourself once a year that would be a great experience and which you would certainly think twice about rewarding yourself with.

Now take your day and year planner and plan ahead putting all the events in and booking those early activities. Your daily routine will be immeasurably improved by the inclusion of your daily habits and the year ahead will both look and be exciting because of your plans. A note here: although the idea of doing this may sound grand or expensive, none of these things necessarily has to cost a great deal, or even anything. Creatively, you can always come up with something to improve the quality of the way you spend time with yourself without it costing a great deal of money. If you have issues around budgeting for these, here is an ideal opportunity to be really creative and make yourself feel better in the process.

FLOW ACTIVITIES

Increased self-confidence and its maintenance are guaranteed by an increase in the level of your flow activities. When you are in flow everything seems effortless. You feel more than equal to the task that you are tackling, time becomes irrelevant and there is a sense of "being in the zone" that precludes interference from negative thoughts. You feel balanced, calm and self-assured. Whatever the specific challenge, you have an innate assurance that you have the skills to deal with it in a confident manner. For athletes, this state is achieved at times when the high level of their training and the repetition of their specific skills allow them to transcend any fear of the challenge in front of them. In a way they move beyond it. Their focus takes them into the realms of invincibility. They have trained so hard and well, they know that not only can they perform to a standard of excellence, but that a specific goal is well within their reach instead of something to aspire to and which may depend on other circumstances for its achievement. Outside the sporting arena, flow activities can feature in our everyday lives. They might range from something you do in your spare time as a hobby, to the execution of some very demanding professional task. As unique individuals, our abilities at different activities are bound to vary wildly. What is easy for one person is more challenging for another. Whether it is hobby or work related, setting the correct balance of your personal Challenge/Skills Ratio will help you to achieve this. If you constantly practise something and at the same time set increasingly higher goals to be achieved to test yourself, the resultant successes and your improved self-efficacy will be matched by indisputable feelings of well being.

This same challenge will have become evident when you formally began Goal Setting and had to identify what you might have to learn or skills that you might have to acquire or improve. Now that you can see the horizon for the first time, (or at least intuitively sense it), you will need to make an informed assessment of what it will take to get you there. Remember that everything you want lies just outside your comfort zone. In order to make progress your participation in this process has to remain active. Nobody coasts to freedom. It need not be a struggle, but it does require effort.

See where your major challenges might be and where you have to improve to a level that will prevent any self-doubts creeping in that will undermine your self-confidence. At the same time, begin to identify which of those activities you engage in allow you to lose track of time. It is the Challenge/Skills Ratio that is important: constantly aim very high while practising everything that is necessary for achieving it beyond the level that is required. If for example, you hate public speaking, but it is an essential skill that you need to acquire, engage a coach to help you with it. Practise rigorously. Rehearse in front of others and ask for constructive feedback. Take advantage of additional opportunities to finesse your skills. Do whatever it takes to ensure that the next time you have an important speaking engagement your focus is not just on successfully conveying your message, but actually pursuing your newly acquired excellence to a new and higher level. Rather than worry about what other people's perceptions of your performance might be, focus instead on improving the already high standard you have achieved. When a task or activity becomes second nature and you have attained a level of accomplishment at it, fear and de-motivating doubts are replaced by the supreme feeling of being bigger than the task. When you have eradicated self-doubt in this way in the areas that might hold you back, your abilities to express yourself more freely grow naturally.

A good example of this would be explained by the training methods that say a professional tennis player might employ. Big competitions often pitch top seeded players against complete unknowns. The sense of occasion as well as the awesome possibilities of a win against a top seeded player can be overwhelming for a new player on the circuit. While they may have talent, they may still be some years from seeing it come to its fruition. Focus therefore has to be very specific and simply encouraging the youngster to play their best game does not help. However, telling them to ignore the score, the overall standard of their game and the response from the crowd and to simply concentrate on returning say every one of their opponent's first serves to the best of their ability puts them into the tunnel zone. No matter what happened with a previous shot or game, the player is solely focused on their present. Whether winning is likely or not, the concentration on this one single aspect of their game can increase efficacy enormously and contribute significantly to their state of flow. They are focused simply on doing one thing to the best of their ability, irrespective of any external validation like winning. The noise of the crowd disappears, no distractions filter through, the player simply operates in suspended time focused uniquely on one single aspect of his game. If we relate this back to the public speaking example, a person seeking to improve their skills at this has the opportunity to concentrate on say counting the length of each pause to heighten the dramatic effect rather than wondering how well their message is being received. Over time this concentration will be expanded into other areas until the confidence they once aspired to becomes a natural part of their being and public speaking no longer holds any fear for them.

In the pursuit of Being, now identify how YOU can move more into flow. Those activities that you now engage in as part of your new status quo are an expression of your Values. Find ways that will stretch your abilities. Practise to a standard that is way beyond even what is expected of you. Expand into the new dimension of supremo. Any challenge, no matter how big, cannot overwhelm you. Be sure to carry out a rigorous assessment of those other tasks that now demand your time. If they are congruent with your newly found expression and already stand out as flow activities, this will become immediately apparent. If they are not, either they need to be replaced or improved to an extent that they no longer present a threat to your progress. Nothing must stand in the way of you and your goals for the future.

YOU AS A VOLCANO!

Think of a volcano. Deep down inside you, pressure is building that seeks an outlet. The tectonic plates of change that slowly grind and shift ease pressure in some places while increasing it in others. When the seismic force of the molten rock and gas of a volcano pushes up something has to give.

The eruption of a volcano is inevitable. The longer and greater its suppression, the more forceful will be the outcome. You are a potential volcano. So are we all. Any long dormant need for expression will eventually find an outlet. The only question to answer is "how" and "where"? Will the force of such a need be an eruption that brings with it devastating consequences as people and familiar structures are buried under a torrent of long-suppressed lava? Might that be in some ways the necessary outcome for your personal growth to be optimised? Or conversely, is it possible that through heightened awareness you can find a natural means to vent the flow and thereby manage the outpouring in a constructive way? A repetition of earlier catastrophe can certainly be avoided if we read the signs and take action.

The diagram on the following page encapsulates all that we have been discussing. It is a volcano - a manageable one at any rate! Once all the elements are in place you have the basis for something that can give full vent to its creative expression. What it represents is a reiteration of those elements that constitute a framework designed to support you. Maintained at its best, it will last and serve you. This does not mean there will be no further change. Your future is as organic as your growth thus far. However, following those inner promptings that urge you to take a certain road and, (if you take it), all the wisdom acquired along the way, means that you will never again experience upheaval of the magnitude that so many experience at mid life. You have shown immense courage to engage with this period in your journey and you will be brave indeed to endure. Your courage now though will ensure your future fulfillment.

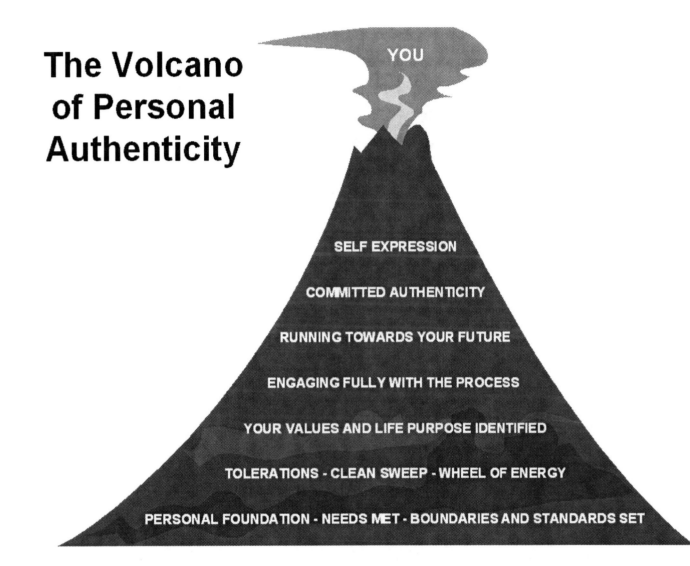

The Volcano of Personal Authenticity

YOU

SELF EXPRESSION

COMMITTED AUTHENTICITY

RUNNING TOWARDS YOUR FUTURE

ENGAGING FULLY WITH THE PROCESS

YOUR VALUES AND LIFE PURPOSE IDENTIFIED

TOLERATIONS - CLEAN SWEEP - WHEEL OF ENERGY

PERSONAL FOUNDATION - NEEDS MET - BOUNDARIES AND STANDARDS SET

Your **Personal Foundation** is the keystone to this structure's solidity. If your **needs** are being met on a full time basis, you have and maintain strong **boundaries** and the **standards** that you set for your conduct are high, you will have all the energy you need to engage in pursuing your own authenticity. To do this will require that your life is free of distraction. Deal with your **Tolerations, Dust Bust** your life of all obstacles to your success. Make sure that the **Wheel of Life** is so balanced that you feel none of the bumps that ordinarily might nudge you off course. Define a compelling **Life Purpose** for yourself. Design a life that encapsulates this and your personal **Values** completely. This is your uniqueness. No one else on the planet can do this in the way that you can if you are completely true to it and trust yourself. And you <u>will</u> trust yourself because you will be running towards your future rather than running away from fear, insecurities and your own perceived lack of substance. Constantly increase your ability to tackle situations both personally and professionally so that the **challenge/skills ratio** is constantly in balance and enables you to engage in Life as an effortless flow activity. When you do this all stresses will become happy challenges and you will lose the fear that previously paralysed you. If you are fully engaged in the process and you have a commitment to the absolute expression of your **authenticity**, then what will be expressed unequivocally, uniquely and powerfully is....

YOU.

I was wondering if I could shape this passion

just as I wanted in solid fire.

I was wondering if the strange combustion of days

the tension of the world inside of me

and the strength of my heart were enough

I was wondering if I could find myself

all that I am in all that I could be

If all the population of stars

would be less than the things I could utter

And the challenge of space in my soul

be filled by the shape I become

- Martin Carter

AUTHOR'S NOTE

I believe this book provides you with the insight into what may have brought you to this place in your life and also powerful tools to take you forward into a future of your choosing. It was my mission in writing the book that as many people as possible would benefit. I want you to be one of them.

What I really, really want for you is for you to be your personal best. Because by being your personal best you CAN and WILL fulfil your potential. If you make it a daily discipline to just do the next right thing, step by step there will be progress. Even on those days when everything seems overwhelming, just keep your eyes on the prize and maintain your commitment to achieving a life worth living. No matter what, keep putting one foot in front of the other. Desire, believe and trust - and you will arrive at your destination.

Bring your unique gifts to the world and live a life that honours you.

- RUSSELL WICKENS

NOTES

NOTES

BIBLIOGRAPHY

Regeneration – Jane Polden
Transform Your Life – Carole Gaskell
Intentional Creation – Lloyd J. Thomas & Michael Anthony
The Heart Aroused – David Whyte
Transitions – William Bridges
Authenticity – David Boyle
Navigating Midlife – Eleanor S. Corlett & Nancy B. Milner
The Life Workbook – Phillip C. McGraw
Build Your Own Rainbow – Barrie Hopson & Mike Scally
Passages - Gail Sheehey
Authentic – Neil Crofts
Flow in Sports – Susan A. Jackson & Mihaly Csikszentmihalyi
Breakthrough Thinking - Gerald Nadler & Shozo Hjibino
Man and Crisis - Jose Ortega y Gasset
The Seasons of a Man's Life – Daniel Levinson
Rites of Passage – Arnold van Gennep
The Ulyssean Adult – John A. B. McLeish
On Death and Dying – Elizabeth Kubler-Ross
Rites and Symbols of Initiation – Mircea Eliade
Women Who Run With the Wolves – Clarissa Pinkola Estes
The Tibetan Book of Living and Dying – Sogyal Rinpoche
Beowulf (translation) Burton Raffel
Beowulf: A Likeness – Randolph Swearer

Printed in the United Kingdom
by Lightning Source UK Ltd.
134842UK00001B/92/A